FOLLOW THE MONEY

*Path to Our Inevitable Economic
Ruin or the End of Global Poverty*

DANIEL GRAY

CONTENTS

THE OVERTURE

Firstly, I Disagree

Our cyclical boom and bust economy is as predictable as it is violently destructive. As you read this, you are likely right now thinking, "Whose side is he on?" I don't want to leave you in suspense: I'm on no one's side. I feel conservative and only vote Democratic. In which economic camp do I reside? Neither! Honestly, I think the Republican policies are cruel, selfish, and frankly, dumb. The Democratic policies are much nicer, but equally dumb.

Now that I've made no friends and lots of enemies, I'd like to challenge some major tenets of Democratic economic principles. They believe that taxing the rich and increasing spending to the poor will make the world a better place, and they believe that education is the key to economic success. I wholeheartedly disagree with these things. I intend on making a full throated defense of my statements, but first I want to be clear that I don't even want to waste any letters right now on stupid Republican economic policies.

While the Democratic economic policies are popular and heartwarming, their constant failures give incredibly stupid economic policies an easy straw man argument. My fellow Democrats, let me ask you a question: What are the ultimate goals or your economic policies? As a black man, who grew up poor, in Harlem, NYC, I hope the goal is to help all people to get a fair shot in our economy. If that is the goal, then you should look for a time when things were great for the constituents that you represent.

I encourage both Democrats and Republicans to consider what made "Black Wall Street" such an affluent economy? Let's consider the facts. Oklahoma didn't become an official state until 1907. While it's true that people of color where flocking there some time before 1907, it's still incredibly curious that a mere 14 years later it would be home to many thousands of affluent former slaves. My Democratic friends, I ask you, how did this happen? With education? No. With taxes? No. These people were left to fend for themselves, and finally in 1921, the anomaly known as Greenwood enraged its white neighbors to the point of a violent riot. Thousands died, goods were looted, and wealth disappeared, never to return. People often look back at this time with shame and wonder how the violence happened. I agree that it was a bad time, but for now let's look past that. How can people go from being slaves on a plantation to wealthy, without government assistance or an extensive education network???

The answer is simple. Follow the money. My research on Greenwood keeps coming up with the quote, "The dollar circulated 36 to 100 times, sometimes taking a year for currency to leave the community."[1] I can't seem to find anywhere that number is substantiated.

I created my own economic theory, and suspected that the economic impact of a dollar spent in Greenwood was at least ten dollars. As no one tracked these things back then, it's hard to tell. But it's hard to deny the reality of our own history. Violent racism forced people who looked like me to buy and sell from each other, creating a template for potential global prosperity.

Before I go on, I need to postulate one thing that will be expounded on at length later. **"Money doesn't come from jobs. Jobs come from money."** I'm tired of hearing about the wealth gap between the races and sexes. It is absolutely relevant, but the solution is neither a Robin Hood tax nor job training. The solution is, and forever will be, economic reciprocity and its multiplicative effect.

Our Imminent Economic Collapse

I so much want to talk about the math, clarify concepts, dispel myths, and talk about history. Every bone in my body wishes me to save the impending collapse of our economy until the end of this book, in a big reveal. It makes logical sense to lay the groundwork to explain in simple English how the financial collapse will happen. I must resist that temptation and submit to the power of the almighty market. This book

---

[1]   The San Francisco Bay View.

is a product and you are my costumer. I hope it all makes sense to you now. If not, continue reading the book and come back later.

While the major political parties wrestle over the best way to move the country forward, an enemy has been creeping up on us and making most of the world's poor: technology. For over a decade, I would tell myself, "The world is one technological advance away from catastrophic economic failure." I stopped saying that to myself as the technology that could collapse the world economy has already arrived. The world has already ended and these jokers in Congress are fighting over tax breaks and food stamps.

What is this earth-shattering technology?? The driverless car! I'm sure you are reading this in disbelief right now. If you aren't as utterly terrified as I am, I will clue you in momentarily. I'd like to reiterate that this isn't some future technology that will be rolling out in the next 25 years. It is happening right now! People can right now buy cars that drive themselves! It is now only a matter of time before most vehicles will be capable of operating on their own.

Let's consider all the facets of this potential dilemma. To make ends meet, I'm currently driving for Uber in NYC. Uber essentially undercut the entire cab market in NYC and most cab companies are struggling. What happens when cars are able to drive themselves? Driverless taxis will put every taxi driver and chauffeur out of work. According to the Bureau of Labor and Statistics, there were 233K taxi drivers and chauffeurs in 2012. Also, their median pay was $22,820. Multiplying these numbers leads to a loss of $531,000,000 in economic activity. I know median isn't the mean, but it is close enough for our purposes.

You may scoff at that and say we can lose that and survive. Those people can get other jobs, right? Cheaper cab services will mean you have more money to spend elsewhere, right? Let's continue the downward spiral.

According to the American Trucking Association, there are approximately 3.5 million professional truck drivers in the US. According to Salary.com, the median income for truckers is $39,446. Given the same math that we used earlier, our economy will suffer $138,000,000,000 in lost economic activity. Will that be made up somehow with lower prices? This is something that we never understood as a country, so I'll bold it: **When you zero out the wealth of individuals, you divide the total wealth in the local economy**.

If automobiles can drive themselves, millions of jobs instantly become obsolete. These people will flood the job market and all the places where they spent their money will take an economic hit. This will be negligible if and only if those who financially profit from the zeroing out of these people spend their profits locally, supplanting the lost economic activity. Wait a minute, you still scoff at the idea that the driverless car is the end of us? All right, let's consider New York City.

Currently, people who work here have no choice of where to live. NYC, like most cities, creates wealth by proximity. Meaning, the wealth multiplies as most people and businesses don't have to go far to spend their money. If the driverless car becomes common, how would that affect NYC? The amount of people who will commute far distances to get to work will skyrocket. NYC is barely affordable for most New Yorkers. How convenient would it be to sleep, eat, work, play games, or do whatever you want on your way to your job? The first to go would be middle income people who could afford the car and would relish the savings. People like teachers, mid-level office workers, sanitation workers, and so on.

These people will be leaving NYC and spending their NYC money elsewhere. The loss of income could certainly prove catastrophic for NYC. You may be thinking, "But the money is still being spent nearby, here in America. It will all recycle somehow." Then I ask you, how does the local grocery store in NYC stay afloat when a percentage of its business is now being spent four hours away? How does the money ever return to NYC? Taxes? No amount of taxes can compensate for the loss of economic activity. Businesses will crumble, property values will plummet, and crime will rise.

If you don't know that the major cities of America are its economic engines, I will explain later. But this is a significant problem for every major city. Less people will be taking public transportation. Less people will be shopping. Less people will attend the local schools. Less people will occupy the housing. Local government budgets will be constrained due to loss of economic activity and the government will do one of two things: raise taxes or cut spending. Both of these fail to address the problem and will exacerbate the issue.

"But," you say, "the markets will even out when the demand of housing further away exceeds the supply of housing! The hand of the market will fix everything." Oh dear, you are so misguided. So the loss of truck and taxi jobs didn't faze you. And the redirection of local wealth also doesn't intimidate you? That is just the beginning with the driverless car. Did you realize that the most valuable real estate in New York City is located near transportation hubs? Why do you think that is?

People just accept that properties near transportation hubs must be valuable, as if it were an immutable axiom. If people aren't limited to how long they can physically drive, or having to rely on public transportation, those places that have the privilege of being located next to a highway off-ramp or a subway station instantly lose their luster. If you combine that with a sharp decline in population, you have a recipe for a housing collapse. "But if prices fall, someone will see value in cheap housing prices!" God, you are stubborn…

How about I put the nail in the coffin? There are two things businesses need to thrive: a competitive advantage and foot traffic. If a significant percentage of people no longer live in NYC, then foot traffic must decrease by a proportional percentage. This is obvious. But what is less obvious is the erosion of business as a whole, in the name of competition. There was a time when there was a variety of local stores. Those small stores could not compete with giant box stores. Then those giant box stores couldn't compete with similar giant box stores using slave labor from around the world. As a result, most neighborhoods are cluttered with the same type of stores right next to each other. In my neighborhood, it's common to see five churches on the same block. Around the corner, there are literally five delis right next to each other. There are two barbershops, two Chinese restaurants, and two laundromats. This has happened because the small stores have lost their competitive advantage.

Most people aren't alarmed when the exact same stores open up next to each other. I am. How can the driverless car exacerbate this? Big box stores of all kinds will lose their competitive advantage. The moment the driverless car becomes widespread, deliveries will become cheaper than ever. How can the mammoth Pathmark stores compete with door to door delivery service at the same or cheaper price? How does Macy's or Walmart compete with distributors shipping products directly to customers? Which local businesses can survive driverless delivery?

Like I said, total economic collapse. And this is just NYC. This same phenomenon will spread all around the country. It will hit the hardest in those states who practice and preach stupid economic policies. Southern states will be stuck in a catch-22. What happens when Americans move to Mexico, but auto-drive themselves to work in their respective southern states? A place like Texas will collapse first because their state government relies almost entirely on local spending, not state taxes. When that begins to slow, they will be left in the uncomfortable position of telling local Texans that they can't do what Texas allows corporations to do. Our economy certainly can't withstand the economic collapse of a bunch of Southern states.

Racism and Genocide Were/Are Inevitable and Natural

There is and has been a campaign of racial shaming in this country for generations. Whether it's deserved or not isn't relevant to me for this point. It's important for us all how and why the brutal past happened, and it isn't because the people in the past were inordinately cruel. Driverless cars are just the beginning for humanity. Economic policies that don't work will eventually have to come face to face with the reality of technology. The same economic conditions that slavery produced will be upon us, possibly within my lifetime.

There will be a day, in the very near future, when androids are capable of replacing human work. All fast food and minimum wage workers will be the first to go when that happens. But will that be the end? Absolutely not! I can foresee a future where androids handle almost all law enforcement, fight all wars, replace all sanitation workers, become short order cooks, and on and on. Apart from highly skilled jobs, androids will essentially zero out the income of billions of people all around the world.

Do you see the similarities with slavery and androids? Although one is morally reprehensible, they both necessarily will engender a violent response due to the catastrophic deflation caused by zeroing out the pay of countless people. Unfortunately, most people don't understand how the flow of wealth works. The real culprits in this system are the ones who profit from the zeroing out of wages and don't spend their wealth in a commensurate way locally. The clear and obvious manifestation of the cause of the deflation, for a rabid crowd, are the individuals or the machines that apparently "took their jobs."

Let me ask you a question. If there were fully functioning androids in the world, do you think you would still have a job? You're a highly skilled individual who can't be easily replaced, you say? Who pays you your salary? Doesn't is come from dog walkers, baby sitters, baristas, fire fighters, and so on? What happens to you when these people get replaced? Can you see yourself ganging up on and destroying androids walking in the street? Can you see yourself demanding legislation prohibiting androids from working in certain fields? Could you see yourself demanding that androids be segregated from the rest of society?

I absolutely don't want to excuse anyone from the brutality of the past. I just want to reaffirm that it is human nature to do whatever it takes to be able to feed your family. Even to this day, people believe in the deflationary effect of "Blackness." The exact conditions of slavery will be upon us again soon. It is my hope that I can shed light on the path that leads to the end of all poverty. But if we continue to have the same fights over bad ideas, then the future is truly bleak.

There are going to be people who question my credentials, morality, and credibility. Before you attempt to attack me, answer me this: Which political party has the solution to the devastating effect of fully functioning androids? Even if America bans the use of androids, companies will employ them all around the world. What happens to the two billion people in China and India who made their bones undercutting the rest of the world's labor force? How do these countries face the deflationary effects of androids? They can't!

Whenever the wealth stops flowing in a local economy, there predictably is some level of civil upheaval. We will be looking at wars, revolutions, civil wars, brutal oppression, and genocide. The future is only bleak, in America, if and only if our parties continue to fight over policies that don't work. I want to reiterate. I don't condone any of the racist or violent acts of the past or the present. I simply understand how and why they happened and continue to happen. How about we follow the money?

Making the Case for Government

There is a vigorous debate going on right now within our government. All sides are fighting about what the role of government should be. Some even suggest that we do away with government and taxes. I'd like to posit this for your edification: This battle has raged ever since the beginning. Much of the fight revolves around taxes, so I'll start there.

Q: Imagine an isolated society, with no government and no taxes. There are many businesses in the society and every person works for or runs a business. Given that a business can only survive if it shows profit, what will the future of this society look like?

A: Since businesses must remain profitable, they are taking more wealth out of the society than they are sending back through wages. The flow of wealth will then begin to pool into a few hands. Wages will decrease, layoffs will increase, and businesses will fail until only a few or one exists. Then there will come a tipping point. There will be a revolution, protests, civil war, genocide, or mass oppression.

This mini mental exercise effectively sums up the rise and fall of every great nation and empire since recorded history. It would please me to no end to thoroughly litigate such a statement, but I must press on. I'll simply state what a government must do, if it is created. <u>A government must maintain a healthy flow of wealth for its nation!</u> Given our first example, the only way that society can function is if there exists a body that taxes everyone equally and spends the tax revenue equally through the society, thus maintaining a healthy flow of wealth.

Some political voices call taxes "redistribution of wealth." It's as if they believe that the wealth is going from deserving to undeserving people. Taxes aren't a burden or a redistribution of wealth. There simply is no other possible way to maintain a healthy economy. If someone can explain that magic of no taxes to me, I'm all ears.

The problem that every single government faces is, "What is an effective tax rate?" The question itself is foolish. Every government is dynamic; if there was a singular number, there would never be any problems. Instead, let's consider all of the ways an economy can crash. <u>A crash happens when the wealth stops flowing</u>.

The reasons why the wealth stops flowing is at least one of these reasons:

1. The rate of change for specific nodes is greater than what is sustainable for the local economy.

2. Wealth is being diverted away from the local economy.
3. Nodes are forcibly removed from the local economy. *(A node is a point where wealth flows through — people, business, or governments.)*

Q: Knowing the rates of change is vital, especially for a complex economy. Let's consider a simple economy with only one store. Everyone works for the store and shops at the store for all things. If this store is profitable, how will this affect the local economy?

A: This local economy will eventually suffer a deep depression and will collapse. Since the company must be profitable, then it must make more money than it pays out to its workers. There could be a mathematically perfect ratio to price of goods and services and salaries, but it's highly unlikely if supply and demand is allowed to work its magic. One day, someone will be fired and that loss of income for the economy will lead to more people being laid off. Or maybe the boss of the company decides to raise the prices or lower the wages since he has a monopoly. The result will be the same.

This is the crux of the debate that rages on in the US. The two sides are technically battling over the size of government, but in actuality they are debating about what to do about our first problem: the rate of change.

On one side, they proclaim the free market! They want to go back to a fantastical time, when a "man can be a man!" I'm not a historian, but I can imagine how it must have been before there existed progressive taxes; wealth must concentrate in the hands of the few in that case.

On the other side, they cry for higher taxes to help those in need. This side feels good, and also has a history of working. But for some reason they are ashamed to state why it works: the flow of wealth. If it's the flow of wealth that you are after, then you don't necessarily need to grow the government.

Tax rates are currently at historic lows, yet Republicans are begging for further tax cuts and deeper government spending cuts. To me, government spending is a secondary factor. The only thing that matters is the flow of wealth.

Let's reconsider our one store society. Applying an income tax to this place will set the stage for the very fight that we are in now. The society's government taxes everyone, and spends at a rate that maintains a sustainable flow of wealth. The owner of the only store looks at the tax as a "redistribution of wealth" and vows to fight it. Yet, every time that he successfully lobbies the government to lower taxes, wages drop, profit drops, and the economy slows.

Now we are stuck with two intransigent sides. On the on hand, they argue that we need to raise taxes to help the poor. On the other hand, they say that the poor are the problem and we can make the economy stronger by not helping them. While I believe that the Democratic position is altruistic, I think it is ultimately short sided. The Republican position is a complete loser and will fail every time. Cutting taxes and spending will **always** lead to an economic collapse.

Next we have wealth being redirected from the local economy. This is something that everyone understands is bad. Yet people are incredibly ignorant about the wealth that they allow to escape the local economy. We all need to understand this one thing. **Stuff is utterly unimportant! The only thing that matters is the wealth passing through each node! The nodes themselves can make more stuff!!!**

Q: Some time ago, I was deeply interested in the stock market. All the financial talkers were elated at the idea that Netflix could expand to China. If the deal went through, I would've likely purchased Netflix shares. I was concerned that Netflix couldn't expand any more and wasn't interested in owning its shares. What troubled me was this: What would happen to China if China said yes?

A: Let's consider that China allowed Netflix to sell to its citizens, tax-free. China has over a billion citizens, but let's be conservative and say Netflix only gets one hundred million Chinese subscribers. If they charge the Chinese the same rate as they charge us, $7 per month, then every month $700,000,000 will be leaving China and filling the Netflix coffers.

The world is connected economically, but I can't see how China can stand that type of loss every month. The money will likely return to the Chinese economy, but the degrees of economic separation and the odds of it returning at an equal or greater amount aren't encouraging.

China would be facing an economic crisis. The sectarian divides that already exist will come to the forefront and blame everything but the real problem, Netflix. Maybe there will be riots, protests, crime, oppression, civil war, or genocide. It's always the same when it comes to what happens when the money disappears. Ideologues arise and play the blame game. No local economy can survive wealth being diverted away from it. Without the wealth, people can't work. Jobs come from the flow of wealth, not from rich people!

Q: In every society, there appears to be some sort of sectarian divide. How do oppression, mass incarceration, economic disparities, and genocide affect a local economy?

A: Any and all action against a group of people within an economy, that affects their ability to add value to the economy, ultimately hurts the economy. Inhibiting or removing a single person from a local economy does nothing but divide the wealth. A few people may prosper from the loss of each node, but the majority of the other nodes will suffer.

There are three things that are the most extreme: genocide, slavery, and mass incarceration. Sometimes these things arise from economic hardship, but they end up creating further economic hardship. Rather than discuss each of these things, I'll simply talk about debtors' prisons since that seems to encapsulate each of them.

Debtors' prisons have risen and fallen many times over the centuries past. When the flow of wealth begins to dry up, people will no longer have the income to pay their debts. Rather than look at society as a whole to figure out why the wealth stopped flowing, some blame the poor.

Consider one person now. This person has difficulty paying his debt. Then he is sent to prison for failure to pay. First, the loss to the society, in the form of this person's earning potential, is immediately felt. This person's family will also be adversely affected. Then every place this person frequented will be affected. In addition, every node will be affected by the loss within some degree of economic separation. Second, it will cost the society money to house this person in prison.

With each person imprisoned, the society faces a mini deflationary event. Each time another person goes to jail, then less money exists in the society, causing more people to default. The Babylonian, Greek, and Roman Empires all employed debtor's prisons. Babylon maintained their prisons until the end. They seemed to like having hordes of people to make public buildings. But they failed to realize that too much of their empire were struggling with poverty. I personally believe that this was a major factor in the Babylonian downfall. Both Greece and Rome outlawed the practice when they realized too many people were going to prison.

Debtors' prisons have proven time and again to be a failure. Yet there are still countries around the world that employ them, including the US. Feel free to search "Debtors' Prison" and peruse at your leisure. Criminalizing poverty is common during an economic crisis. But proponents of such a policy fail to understand that it costs the economy more money to punish people for being poor. The real issue is the flow of wealth.

Then we have the lessor segregation tactics in societies: discrimination, blocking immigration, and the prison-industrial complex. While I call these less than something like genocide, I mean that it's less only in its application. The result is nonetheless the same. As a black male, who grew up in Harlem, I saw firsthand what people like me have to go through on a daily basis. There are many things to rail about, but instead I'll focus on the illegal immigrants. All of the issues are in fact the same.

These immigrants can be a boon to our economy, if we let them. What I mean is, if they are actually afforded the ability to make as much as everyone else. The immigration debate that is going on in Congress now is really about the idea that wealth is limited. Some people believe that if these immigrants have legal status, they will take money away from "real Americans." There are people that want the immigrants to remain a shadow class and make less money than everyone else.

The problem is the fact that they are making less than everyone else is the problem. Having a subculture of people making less than everyone else is in fact a deflationary event that must spread throughout the nation. I'm amazed that the US is still standing considering the millions of illegal immigrants working for slave wages and the mass incarceration of the descendants of slaves. At the heart of it, no economy can survive the diminished abilities of its nodes. Yet the least among them seem to always be blamed for the economic woes.

The Key to Financial Freedom and Prosperity

Q: What is at the root of the world's economic problems?

A: Simply put, the flow of wealth.

There is a false idea that if some prosper then others must suffer. That idea is a self-fulfilling prophecy until the idea totally collapses. The truth is, while actual money is limited, wealth is unlimited. What we call wealth is always in constant motion. The idea called wealth is in fact a sum of three things: ability, rate of change, and amount in circulation. People, businesses, and governments all operate under these three forces. For the purposes of creating a unified theory, I'll call people, business, and governments nodes. Then the equation is the flow of wealth equals the sum of the ability of each node, the rate wealth passes through each node, and the amount of money that is currently passing through each node.

Thus, the sum of this nation's wealth is the aggregate of each node's ability, rate of change, and amount of change. Changing any of these three things will affect the nation's wealth. It is then incumbent upon the nation to maintain a database on each node. Most of this information already exists at the IRS. The government seems to only focus on the ability of the nodes. As if it is the only factor in the wealth of the nation. It's true that highly skilled workers add great value to a nation's wealth. Also, innovative businesses add great value to the nation. But it is just as important to know how quickly money is changing hands and how large the amounts of money are. Ignorance of this vital information is inexcusable.

Another factor involving the flow of wealth is where each node directs the flow. The direction of the flow of wealth can either grow or destroy a local economy. It is beyond unavoidable then, that the nation should become aware and make public the direction of each node's flow of wealth. Understanding how important these things are, I recommend the government create a new office. This office's task is to track and make relatively public this vital data.

Collecting and analyzing this data is extremely important. Yet, people who cling to the idea that some are born to be less need to openly fight it. I can only imagine the ridiculous arguments for not analyzing the information that we already have. Though they can never openly admit it, the reason for fighting this plan is that it immediately assigns value to each and every node. In addition to that value, there will be a mathematical correlation between each and every node. The immigration fight will have no basis in reality, the prison industrial complex will be exposed as an epic fail, and the bankruptcy of Detroit will be seen as self-destructive.

Let's quickly discuss Detroit, since it is the most imminent threat to the nation's economy. At the heart of the Detroit debacle is the application of the original idea that some are born better than others. Michigan was the birthplace of the Labor Movement. While there were many apparent gains for the worker during that time, the Labor Movement unfortunately did nothing about the idea the caused them to act. Many cities in Michigan were snuffed out due to divestment. The failure of Detroit, to me, is the resulting counter-assault after the Civil Rights and Labor Movements. Listening to the reasoning for the proponents for letting Detroit go bankrupt, I hear that it's a failure of Unions and Democratic principles, and also I hear that the people who remain are worthless. The people that live in Detroit are mainly people of color.

When I think about this issue, it reminds me of the two beings on a person's shoulders whispering in his ears. But in this case, one isn't a devil or an angel; they both are dingbats. On the one hand, one is telling the person to shoot off one of his testicles. "It's a useless testicle!" it says. The other one is saying, "I know this testicle hasn't been doing well, but it's still a nice testicle." And the guy holding the gun to his testicle is totally confused about what to do. Blowing off one of our testicles will hurt like hell and it might kill us!

Let's assume that this public office already exists and is sending data about each and every node. I'd be able to download an app on my smartphone to express this data. In order to understand this data, consider for a moment your next door neighbor. If your next door neighbor lost his job and health, would that affect your local economy? A person in a city like New York might not directly feel it. But in a small town of a hundred people, everyone will miss the loss of your neighbor's income. The opposite is also true. In a small town of a hundred, if your neighbor hits the lottery, it will positively impact your local economy. What people fail to realize is that we are all connected by various degrees of economic separation.

Let's consider my smartphone now. I'm concerned about the situation in Detroit and want to know how it will affect my personal economy. It will be a matter of clicking a few buttons. The government has tracked all transactions there are in the nation and has connected them to the node that is me. I can choose a singular person and glean some important information. First, how many degrees of economic separation are there between me and that person? What percentage is the chance that wealth will flow from that person to me and the amount of wealth that could flow to me? The app will also allow me to add up all nodes in the city of Detroit and analyze the possibilities for the entire city.

Here is the reason why defenders of the original idea need to fight this information at all costs. There will be an actual number for the degrees of economic separation between a singular node anywhere in the nation and the entire city of Detroit; the probability that a percentage of the wealth of Detroit reaches a particular node anywhere in the US is definitely not zero, and finally the amount of wealth that could flow from Detroit to a specific node in the US isn't zero either. With this mathematical model, it will be proof that these people have actual value to each citizen and business. In addition, it will be proof that a prosperous Detroit would lead to a prosperous nation.

I understand what conservatives think would happen in Detroit. They believe that there will be a time of economic despair, and then investors will swoop in to get amazing deals. When the process of gentrification takes place, investors can sit back and watch their investments grow. That process seems to have worked wonders in the past, and it reinforces that idea that some people are the cause of economic problems. Unfortunately, such a process has never happened on a grand scale. I don't think it will play out the way some would wish it.

I would then return to my smartphone app. Some apps would allow me to increase and decrease the flow of wealth in Detroit, to see how it would affect me personally. Again, it would prove that as the flow of wealth increases in Detroit, so does my personal economy. The negative would be true as well. There would be another function on this app. It would show me a map of Detroit's degrees of economic separation from the rest of the country, along with the rates and amounts of change. Such a map would look like decreasing waves emanating from Detroit.

From this map, we can see Detroit's connection to all the surrounding nodes. From here we can deduce the result from a default of one of the country's largest cities. The flow of wealth will cease from the city and in turn will cease for many of its inhabitants. This is the rapid spread of deflation. Once these nodes are removed from the flow, then related businesses will suffer and begin to lay off its workforce. Those who are laid off represent their own nodes as well. Removing these people from the flow of wealth will cause a cascading affect. The wealth of the entire nation will be divided.

Even flirting with the idea of letting Detroit go bankrupt is complete lunacy. It could well mean the end of our country. Feel free to examine all of the other "great" countries who also removed large segments of the population from the flow of wealth. That was the undoing of them all. But by all means, do what you think is right.

The most damning thing this app would show the country is why Detroit is going bankrupt. It would show that wealth is flowing out of Detroit and not returning. There is no amount of spending or taxation that will save a local economy from a redirection of wealth.

This may seem like a heavy political lift, but it isn't. We shall see later how indispensable more information is. This is the future of economics, and conservatives always tend to fight the future. I started this process attempting to understand how our government works, and ended up finding the key to liberating all oppressed people. There are other things that I may suggest that sound appealing, but they will never compare to a real-time financial tracking system.

If anyone has any concerns about privacy, then individual nodes can have anonymity. They can share their information with their friends. Even then, individual transactions won't be listed, only statistics relative to other nodes. Businesses and local governments will be searchable. The possibilities are too numerous to count. I need to keep this short so as not to tune you out. **But remember, this is the key!**

How Wealth Actually Multiplies

"We may congratulate ourselves that this cruel war is nearing its end. It has cost a vast amount of treasure and blood...It has indeed been a trying hour for the Republic; but I see in the near future a crisis approaching that unnerves me and causes me to tremble for the safety of my country. As a result

of the war, corporations have been enthroned and an era of corruption in high places will follow, and the money power of the country will endeavor to prolong its reign by working upon the prejudices of the people until all wealth is aggregated in a few hands and the Republic is destroyed. I feel at this moment more anxiety for the safety of my country than ever before, even in the midst of war. God grant that my suspicions may prove groundless.[2] Abraham Lincoln

There is a considerable amount of misinformation regarding how money actually works. I'd like to think that I'm thorough, but I have a sense that I need to explain how wealth multiplies and divides as people buy and sell goods and services. First, let's define and understand what reciprocity is.

Reciprocity
1. A reciprocal condition or relationship.
2. A mutual or cooperative interchange of favors or privileges, especially the exchange of rights or privileges of trade between nations.

My Wealth Equation

The sum of this nation's wealth is the aggregate of each node's ability, rate of change, and amount of change. Changing any of these three things will affect the nation's wealth.

Let's consider the Federal Government and how it gets revenues. The current federal budget seems astronomical. When numbers reach the hundreds of billions of dollars, people simply tune out. I don't think our brains are normally supposed to operate with such numbers. In any case, the actual number isn't relevant. All that we need to understand is that the Federal Government has reciprocity with nearly every node in the nation. Meaning that, almost every time money goes from one node

---

[2]   U.S. President Abraham Lincoln, Nov. 21, 1864 (letter to Col. William F. Elkins)

to another, the Federal Government gets a portion of the money and spends that money in a way that affects each node.

Let's assume that the tracking system that we previously spoke of exists. This means every node has an idea of how other nodes affect their personal economy. This information will be especially useful to the Federal Government. Now let's observe how a dollar is actually multiplied by changing hands.

There exists at least one government contractor. It is also true that this contractor gets paid directly from the Federal Government. It is also true that for every dollar that the contractor receives from the government, this contractor is required to pay taxes to the Federal Government. So then, at least one dollar is returned to the Federal Government for further use. With this simple exercise, we can see that at least one dollar in the annual federal budget is a repeat. The real question the Federal Government should want to know is, What was the rate in which the dollar repeated?

There are many people who attempt to look at the federal budget like a personal budget with a fixed income. With this simple example, we can see that it's just not the case. Especially considering EVERY government employee and contractor pays taxes. This means that a considerable amount of the budget is repeat dollars.

Since we have a real-time tracking system in place, the Federal Government can inspect every place it directs its money. Each node will have various levels of reciprocity, or various chances of wealth returning and at various rates. In the past, price and ability was the only factor. Now, by simply choosing the different contractors, the federal budget could potentially be increased by a significant amount! We didn't raise taxes or cut spending, yet the budget was increased significantly.

A real-time tracking system will directly benefit any node that doesn't have a fixed income, and indirectly affect every node. Any business can simply choose to deal with other nodes if and only if the nodes have a high reciprocity with them, given any number of degrees of economic separation. With good reciprocity, every dollar spent would have a strong chance of returning. It will also be clear that some businesses have a negative reciprocity. Meaning, it actually costs money to do business with them.

Recently, the SNAP program was significantly cut. Both sides have dug in and are talking past each other. One thing that the Democrats repeatedly said was this: "SNAP helps to boost the economy."

Fact: Every \$1 in SNAP benefits generates \$1.73 in economic activity. (Source: Moody's)

It is also a fact that when poor people receive any money, they spend it right away. This is true for SNAP dollars and regular dollars as well. Considering My Wealth Equation, when the SNAP dollars enter the local economy, they pass through the poor nodes right away, then go to local store owners. Instantly, when one SNAP dollar goes through a node, a dollar of work is purchased from a food vendor. There is no slippage in reciprocity from the poor SNAP recipients and the store owners. Next, that dollar begins to exchange many hands, with various reciprocal effects on the local economy. How is it that, "Every \$1 in SNAP benefits generates \$1.73 in economic activity?" It's simple math. The first dollar of economic activity comes from the SNAP recipient. The following amount is the aggregate of tax dodging, outsourcing, and flowing to areas with relative deflation as money exchanges hands to infinity. It would be better if every SNAP dollar produced \$10 of economic activity.

Contrary to popular belief, the poor actually multiply the nation's wealth. This is because they usually spend all the money that comes into their possession. This is why, above all things, I think the real-time tracking system is vital. Then everyone would see that the very groups that they blame for all the nation's problems actually have the highest reciprocity to the rest of the nation.

What "smart" people talk about is "fear" and "uncertainty." They say the problem with the economy is that people aren't spending. Or they combine the factors, saying that people are afraid so they don't spend. When, in reality, wealth is being diverted, thus dividing the wealth. When there is no more money, people can't work.

It's a shame that we think in this manner. It will always be the case that when wealth is diverted, there will be less money for people to work for. The economy eventually crashes and the people with all the money point their fingers at everyone else. With every crash, the government steps in and spends a great deal. While I'm not against a bailout, I'm against allowing the system to crash. There are far too many nodes in our society with negative reciprocity with everyone else. No system can survive repeated heart attacks.

If it were the law that every non-public node must maintain a certain level of financial reciprocity with nodes here and abroad, it would have the same financial outcomes as Greenwood, Oklahoma at the beginning of the 1900s. I have no idea what it would mean if every dollar spent meant economic activity of thirty or more dollars. I'm excited to one day find out.

Constructing the United States

America Was Not Built on the Backs of Slaves!

"History is written by the Victors." Winston Churchill

Americans often thump their chests and claim how great we are as a people. There is a grand fantasy of how poor Europeans came to this land in search of freedom and a better life, and "pulled themselves up by their own bootstraps." There is an equally foolish assumption that, "America was built on the backs of slaves." In effect, there are two competing versions of the history of the country, and the line of demarcation between the two is race.

Well, then. I gladly challenge the proponents of these historical perspectives to show me a modern example of your version of events. Where in the world has a similar thing ever happened? Do you believe that your whiteness can transform a jungle into a prosperous community? Please explain to me how such a thing would work. If someone could step forward and demonstrate how poor white people moving to a jungle could create a vibrant economy, then that person would be insanely wealthy.

Along the same vein, when and where in history did slavery make a nation wealthy? According to the Walk Free Foundation, there are an estimated 35.8 million slaves in the world today. Are the countries with the most slaves oozing with wealth? Here are countries with the most slaves in them, from most to least: India, China, Pakistan, Uzbekistan, Russia, Nigeria, Democratic Republic of Congo, Indonesia, Bangladesh, and Thailand.[3] These countries are easily some of the poorest in the

---

[3]   2014 Global Slavery Index

world. Slavery isn't, and has never been, at all profitable. On the contrary, slavery makes most people in that entire community poor.

How was America built? How did it become the nation it is? **America was built on the backs of European countries, during a time when European empires divided and pillaged the planet amongst themselves.** America was created by the arrogance and ignorance of the Royalty of Europe. This arrogance and stupidity ultimately led to the downfall of most monarchies and empires. Let us follow the money.

The "Great Migration"

In the early 1600s, as European Empires traveled the world claiming locations as their own by force, the royalty of Europe had a brilliant idea. Instead of directly governing over the lands they seized, as the Romans did before them, they would send corporations in their stead and charge those corporations various taxes. In fact, in 1600, the world's first limited liability corporation was the East India Company.

There were many such companies in America over time. But they were nothing compared to the East India Company. The biggest difference between the East India Company and the American companies was that no one wanted to live in a jungle that was across a vast ocean and surrounded by hostile natives. American businessmen set up plantations with the vast open lands and essentially undercut prices in Europe.

The first successful English corporation in America was called the Virginia Company. It was a joint stock company chartered by King James 1 in 1606. It was divided into two companies: the Virginia Company of Plymouth, and the Virginia Company of London. The Plymouth division failed quickly, but the London company survived.

The company's financial backers enlisted the help of 144 men in an expedition for finding gold. Most of the men were indentured slaves. This is how the corporation kept costs down. The men would work for the company for a period of time and would be set free if profits were made or the time expired. The history books call these people "Adventurers." From the moment corporations were let loose on the world, their sole purpose was to get profits at any cost. These so called adventurers did nothing but murder, steal, and enslave.

The trials and tribulations of these individuals are not relevant to us here. What is relevant is the great migration. The Virginia Company established Jamestown, and the population grew rapidly from a handful of people to 4500 by 1623. This was known as the Great Migration.

Our "great" nation was started by a corporation seeking gold. Then they decided to grow tobacco and kidnap natives to sell in Europe. As with any modern corporation, if what you did shows a profit, then do it some more. The company used slave labor, and "free" land to produce goods for sale. When others saw that profits were made, more "adventurers" decided to follow in the Virginia Company's footsteps.

This history, and much more, is available to those who wish to understand America's real past. For example, the people who followed the Virginia Company were the Puritans. I've only known the Pollyanna version of Thanksgiving from school and stories. The real truth is heart-wrenching. The bloody past is important to know, but for our purposes it is just extra.

What we have is the germ for the American economy. Corporations and individuals, seeking to increase their wealth and status, plundered the natives and the land of America. Then they sold the goods in Europe. Unfortunately, for the British Empire, they were blinded by their own greatness. They never stopped to think about what was actually happening. The slave labor in America was undercutting the prices for goods sold at home. We will consider that in depth in a moment. First let's see how brutal American slavery began.

The ~~Triangle~~ "V" Slave Trade

Slavery in the 1600s was much as it is now. People were duped into believing they would be getting a better life, only to realize that they are indebted to a person or corporation. In that corporation's great benevolence, they offer the poor sucker the chance to work off their debts. Once the debts are paid, then they were free to go. It was and is usually the case that the slave will never go free.

The first Africans to arrive in America were aboard the Dutch ship, the White Lion, in 1619. The slaves were traded for food and supplies and the Virginia company employed them as indentured servants, in the same way that some Europeans were enslaved. The slavery scheme was prevalent all around the world. "Adventurers" saw trading people as quick profit. As a result, the people of the Virginia Company regularly raided Native camps and kidnapped them to be sold in Europe as indentured servants.

In 1622, the Natives struck back, killing 347 people in what is called the Jamestown Massacre. There was debate among investors in the Virginia Company as to whether or not the company should continue, since profits had ceased. In 1624, the King simply dissolved the Company and incorporated Virginia as a royal colony. Then the natives had to deal directly with the Royal army, and the colony/company was free to expand.

England, during this time, was already suffering the effects of prolonged deflationary factors. Its obsession with status and primogeniture created stark financial imbalances. Primogeniture is the right of succession to the eldest son. With all of its military might, England suffered from a weak economy, low wages, and high unemployment. I suspect that the King himself may have started the "America is the land of milk and honey" campaign. It apparently killed two birds with one stone. The unemployed and estate-less could go to America and work as slaves, thus making profits for the crown and getting rid of unsightly people.

Both ideas were incredibly dumb. First, the people are the ones that multiply the wealth. There is no local economy that can survive a significant loss of its population. When you lose those people, you lose their economic activity. Secondly, having the population buy cheap American goods further exacerbated matters, as the money sent to America only returned as a small percentage to the Crown. By following the money, we can clearly see that the people in England must have suffered an incredible deflationary event. **If the money continuously flows in one direction, there will always be protests, wars, revolutions, and genocides**. This happens without fail, as the people want to find a way to feed their families. England was no exception.

In 1642, there was a civil war in England. The fight was ultimately between the King and the Parliament. In 1649, Charles 1 was beheaded and many of the Royalists were persecuted. The Royals fled to America and ruled Virginia, and were known as the Tidewater Aristocracy.

In 1676 there was an armed rebellion in Virginia, called the Bacon's Rebellion. Nathaniel Bacon, the leader of the rebellion, was frustrated by the treatment he was receiving by the ruling class. The rebellion was suppressed by a passing armed merchant ship loyal to the crown. When a similar rebellion took place in Maryland within a year, the ruling class devised a plan to keep the indentured servants from revolting. Instead of giving in to the demands of the people, they divided them. They took rights away from the African born indentured servants. They were brutalized and treated as worthless.

While it is true that African slaves did work for free, so did most of everyone else. It was merely a tactic to keep the majority of the workers in line. For a long time it didn't make any sense to me why people would go through the trouble of going to Africa, kidnapping people, and letting most of them die on the way to America. It only makes sense if you consider what the Europeans had to go through. They were packed into boats like sardines, with only the clothes on their backs, and indentured to the people who sponsored their trip. Many of them died on the way to America as well. The brutal voyage to America was apparently made better for the Europeans, because those "other" people had it worse. Also, the majority of white slaves were likely appalled and terrified at the sight of the brutal conditions of the blacks.

History books say that Europeans were fleeing religious persecution. While that may be true, it makes little sense. Scores of people won't leave a place because of general mistreatment. The Catholic Church was brutal, but it wasn't mass murdering Europeans. The reality is, people were fleeing extreme poverty in hopes that they could have a better life. This very same thing happens today. Individuals leave a place where the wealth isn't flowing, to go where they believe the wealth is flowing.

This created what is taught in history books as the "Triangle Slave Trade." Unfortunately, I have to disagree again with these whitewashed history books. There existed a "triangle" for a short time. Slaves were kidnapped from Africa, sold to America, and American raw materials produced by slave labor were sold to Europe. Europe did, for a time, send finished goods to Africa in exchange for slaves. Eventually that production was supplanted by American workers in the North.

Effectively, the V slave trade tilted the economic playing field into America's favor. Only leaders in America profited. American goods undercut European goods, making the people poor. The people wanting to not be poor fled to the "land of milk and honey," only to be slightly better than African slaves. When the people left, it hurt the European economies further due to the loss of economic activity. This is a vicious cycle that always leads to bloodshed.

A Generation of Bloodshed

People flocked to America from every region of Europe to get a piece of the action. I'm not entirely sure how long indentured servitude continued for the European immigrants, but in time it kind of just faded away. Nonetheless, slave wages still persisted. The southern states and the Caribbean became the place where things like cotton, sugar, tea, and tobacco were grown. In the northern states, these goods were processed then shipped to ports in New York City bound for Europe. Most of the Europeans immigrated to the northern states, as it was very difficult to compete with the slaves in the South.

There is considerable debate amongst historians about what caused the following years of global strife, but this is clear as day to me. The colonies went from a few thousand people to hundreds of thousands, with one clear goal: sell cheap goods to Europe and make profits. Whenever money flows in one direction, eventually the wealth stops flowing. When the wealth stops flowing, on a global scale, there is usually a global conflict.

The Seven Years' War took place between 1754 and 1763. In my opinion, this should've been called World War One. It involved Europe, North America, Central America, West Africa, India, and the Philippines. In some sense it was a war between England and France for worldwide dominance. Whatever the players, stated causes, or potential catalysts, the fact is Europe and the world as a whole were ripe for conflict. It's like blaming a brushfire on the guy who threw his cigarette out his car window. While it may be true that the actual fire came from the cigarette, it shouldn't be given all the credit for the blaze. Drought and scorching temperatures set the stage for any disturbance to start the brushfire.

Likewise, European countries had to compete with slave wage goods and a significant decrease in their populations. There are, of course, other factors, but the biggest issue that no one even mentions is American slavery. Various empires made and broke treaties. When the war ended, over a million people died.

This war was important to England because it gained more territory in America, thus continuing our construction of this great country. But the mood of the British Empire had changed towards America after the Seven Years' War. Possibly, someone noticed that American goods were wreaking havoc on domestic businesses. Maybe someone realized that people leaving the country and never returning wasn't good. We can only glean clues from policies instituted by the Empire.

The Glorious Revolution of the Corporations

Many say that the American Revolution happened because of onerous taxes levied upon the people of the colonies. And that because of a large war debt, from the Seven Years' War, the British Empire sought to increase taxes on the colonies. On the surface that seems to make sense. But a deeper look at matters will color things differently.

In the sixteenth century, the British Empire adopted the economic theory known as mercantilism. Mercantilism is an economic policy aimed at accumulating monetary reserves through a positive trade balance. So the British Empire began tracking the gold — the currency at the time — entering and leaving the empire. In 1651, the British Empire put the Navigation Acts into effect. These were a series of laws aimed at maximizing the Empire's trade surplus. The Navigation Acts attempted to maintain a healthy flow of gold within its territories. It prohibited the colonies from trading directly with foreign governments and their colonies. It used tariffs and other means to attempt to balance trade. These laws were mostly obeyed for a long while in America. In time, American smugglers realized that they could multiply their profits by simply ignoring the British Empire and trading with whom they wished.

The Molasses Act of 1733 was a watershed moment for the colonies of every empire. This Act imposed a tax of six pence per gallon on imports of molasses from non-British colonies. The British Empire clearly wanted to protect its assets in the Caribbean. There were likely pencil pushers in London who noticed a trade imbalance and recommended this law. While it makes sense on paper, there was no way to enforce this law. All of the colonies ignored the Molasses Act. In the off chance a smuggler happened upon a British warship patrolling the seas, the smuggler would simply bribe the captains of those ships.

After 1733, the colonies adopted the idea of "free trade." The American Revolution started long before 1776. It started when the British Empire began to track its trade balances and see losses in the Americas. The first attempt to maintain a positive trade balance nominally worked. The next attempt, the Molasses Act, was viewed as onerous and unenforceable. To this day, business people sing the praises of free trade on the mountaintops, as if the British Empire is still attempting to impose tariffs.

In an attempt to crack down on smugglers and bribery, the Parliament passed the Revenues Act in 1762. They got rid of absentee customs officials and gave the Navy enhanced powers. The Navy was charged with apprehending and detaining smugglers, using search warrants called "writs of assistance." These warrants allowed custom collectors to search any boat or house for smuggled goods.

In 1768, customs officials seized John Hancock's ship, in Boston, on charges of smuggling wine. Hancock was one of the wealthiest Americans, and it is well known that Hancock made his wealth smuggling molasses, tea, tobacco, rum and wine. Hancock was also known for his radical political views. I think Hancock's ship was targeted specifically due to him being a famous smuggler and political upstart.

When this ship was impounded, the Sons of Liberty took to the streets in protest. The Sons of Liberty notably included Samuel Adams, John Hancock, Patrick Henry, Paul Revere, and Joseph Warren. John Hancock was the financier of the group. The protest started out peacefully, then became violent. They attacked the customs officials and the customs house. The British government sent 700 troops to stop the rioting.

This was the beginning of the revolution. This riot was started and financed by John Hancock. Most history books like to imply that it happened spontaneously. The truth is, trade tariffs didn't affect the average citizen. In fact, most people were incredibly poor and more than likely slaves. Hancock's goods were bound for Europe. What happened is that a wealthy man paid people to protest in his favor. Then poor opportunists joined into the ensuing riot. Most people simply had no skin in the game.

Most Americans worked long hours for little or no pay. Even many of the Sons of Liberty were incredibly poor. What's more, is that these regulations were for the benefit of the people. Why would poor people protest the right to be able to trade with French colonies? The only person who had any real skin in the game was John Hancock.

Next the Parliament passed the Currencies Act in 1764. This was an attempt by the British Empire to regulate paper money issued by the colonies in America. The colonies were all run by local corporations and issued their own currencies. British merchants and creditors were regularly being paid with depreciated colonial currency. In America, the only law was to make profits as quickly as you could. Paying for goods and services with money you could print yourself was one example of that. This policy was another one of the "grievances" that are cited as a cause for the American Revolution. Again, the only people this affected were the people purposely devaluing the local currency for personal gain.

Next Parliament passed the Sugar Act of 1764. This was just like the Molasses Act, except the tariff was three pence per gallon and increased enforcement measures. To be clear, this was a tax on foreign molasses. Many cite this as a reason to revolt, but it seems quite reasonable from my perspective. Molasses from the other colonies were cheaper than the British colonies' molasses. The British Empire sought to protect the colonies from being undercut by the French, Dutch, and Spanish molasses. The only people who would be upset at this are the people who profit from a tilted playing field.

The Stamp Act of 1765 was next. This was a genuinely stupid tax. It declared that any paper used in the colonies must be stamped paper produced in London. The reasoning for this tax was to "pay for the troops" stationed in the colonies. Clearly the British Empire needed to raise funds in order to maintain a trade balance. After the Seven Years' War, the British Empire was likely making little to no money from its supposed colonies. Every attempt at collecting revenue seemed to fail. The Stamp Act was no exception.

Protests and demonstrations, initiated by the group Sons of Liberty, were often violent and destructive. The Stamp Act gave the group a way for average people to identify with them. Parliament repealed the Stamp Act in 1766, due to pressure from its own merchants' complaints about protests.

Next Parliament passed the Townsend Act in 1767. The stated purpose of the act was to pay the salary of the judges and governors. Effectively, it was the same molasses/sugar tax from before but with more reasoning and stricter enforcement. This was again met with staged violent protests. Which ultimately led to the Boston Massacre in 1770. It may seem like I'm making light of this issue. Far from it. Five people did die, but they were paid agitators who were protesting a tax that likely didn't affect them. The same thing happens all around the world; when you incite violent protest, you get met with armed resistance from those charged to maintain order.

The Boston Massacre was propagandized by the Sons of Liberty. Paul Revere engraved the famous "The Fruits of Arbitrary Power, or the Bloody Massacre," to be printed and distributed to all of the colonies. It is purely speculative to say that John Hancock commissioned, printed, and distributed the engraving. But honestly, who financed that piece of propaganda? Really, I would like to know.

The supposed final straw was the Tea Act of 1773. The East India Company had eight million pounds of unsold tea and the Parliament decided to export the tea directly to America, duty-free. The British Empire offered to sell the colonies cheap tea. The only people who would be affected by this were the companies/businessmen in the business of tea selling; for example, John Hancock. On December 16, 1773, the Sons of Liberty again staged another political demonstration in Boston: the Boston Tea Party. The Sons of Liberty boarded an East India Company ship and tossed the tea into the Boston Harbor, destroying the tea. This of course led to a response by the authorities. But somehow this led to a nationwide revolt?

In 1774, Parliament passed the Coercive Acts in response to the Boston Tea Party. Massachusetts lost its right to self-governance through these acts. This was what supposedly banded all of the colonies together, in outrage, to fight a war against the most powerful empire on the planet?

If you look at it objectively, you'd see that the British Empire is simply losing money on its colonial investments. The Empire set up the colonies in a way similar to the companies that proceeded them. But the companies didn't want to pay any taxes. American companies didn't see any point in paying taxes and sought to undercut all the prices for goods sold in Europe. American smuggling of slave produced goods were hurting the local British economy. Be honest, if you ruled the British Empire, would you have done any differently?

I believe that the British realized the havoc slave produced goods were having on their economy. And sentiment towards American made goods began to shift. In 1771, a slave named James Somerset escaped from his master, who was traveling in England. He was captured and was to be sent to the British Colony of Jamaica to be sold. Abolitionists petitioned the court on his behalf and The Chief Justice of the King's Bench, Lord Mansfield, said this in his ruling in 1772:

> *The state of slavery is of such a nature, that it is incapable of being introduced on any reasons, moral or political; but only positive law, which preserves its force long after the reasons, occasion, and time itself from whence it was created, is erased from memory: it's so odious, that nothing can be suffered to support it, but positive law. Whatever inconveniences, therefore, may follow from a decision, I cannot say this case is allowed or approved by the law of England; and therefore the black must be discharged.*

The Chief Justice said slavery wasn't approved by the law of England? The British Empire started the colonies with slavery, and they made the slave trade possible! This ruling sent shockwaves all throughout the colonies. It was a signal that the British Empire may regulate or outlaw slavery altogether. Slavery gave the American companies its competitive advantage. Without slaves, the vast profits would cease. By 1774, the First Continental Congress met, and by 1775 the Congress declared independence.

It may seem like I'm brushing over these monumental events in our history. It quite honestly feels like an insult to my intelligence to believe that these independent states would band together because the British Empire punished Massachusetts. To say that this was an uprising by the populace is also absurd.

I'm not for or against the British Empire. It's just that my history books and classes left out some important details. For example, who financed the Revolutionary Army? Were the men fighting being paid? How did they eat and who paid for their weapons? Were their goals similar to the goals of the Sons of Liberty?

John Hancock likely financed part of the Revolution, but the bulk of the war effort came in the form of lending from the French Empire, through Haym Salomon. Without the French, the American Revolution would have never happened. The American Revolution was ultimately a continuation of the Seven Years' War, and the French were still bitter about the loss.

The decisive battle was the battle of Yorktown in 1781. George Washington was in command of 17,000 French and American troops. The British contingent of 9000 were hemmed in by a fleet of French ships and Washington's army. That was the end of fighting in America and the US was recognized as a free and independent nation a year later.

A confluence of events ultimately created America. The first was the wealthy businessmen's desire not to pay taxes but still receive protection from the Empire. Next was the French's desire for payback from the loss to Britain. Finally, the desire to have a balanced economy set off red flags in the British Empire; slavery was hurting Britain. Did the British really surrender or did they just give up trying? The American colonies weren't profitable to the Empire, so why were they fighting so hard for it in the first place? Pride?

In case there was any confusion as to who revolted in America, only white male property owners were allowed to vote and ultimately hold office. This was written into the Constitution.

Contrast to a Real Revolution

After the Seven Years' War and the American Revolution, the French were on the brink of financial collapse. There are many theories on why the French economy was so bad. I would like to not entertain any of them. I'd simply like to follow the money. In the mid-1700s, everyone was taxed, except royalty and the clergy. Given that these two groups essentially owned most of the means of production, this set up a bottleneck in terms of the flow of wealth. Simply put, wealth flowed into the direction of the royals and clergy and it was up to those people to spend the money they made.

That is just the beginning. France had adopted the system of mercantilism in the past, but stopped following its tenets along the way. The French had successfully fought for the American's right to "free trade." The French, in their haste to best Britain, allowed the free trade of slave goods in their markets. I believe, above all else, that this made the people desperately poor. Chances are, most of the people were clothed in American slave produced clothing, drinking slave produced wine, smoking slave produced tobacco, and on and on. How does any of that wealth ever return to the people of France?

I'm baffled about how no one ever suggested that a contributing cause of the French financial crisis, before the revolution, was cheap American goods. The very same deflationary factors are happening today all around the world. Look what happens when Walmart enters a small town, or check out the Free-Trade zones in Mexico. Poverty and desolation always follow this type of deflation. France was no exception.

Now the Monarchy, strapped for cash, was stuck with a difficult choice. In fact, it is almost always the same choice after major deflationary events. In 1786, France proposed a tax on the wealthy. While the wealthy debated whether or not this tax would change anything, the people revolted in 1789.

Historians look at the French Revolution as a great moment in history. It is true that it essentially ended monarchies and theocracies around the world and replaced them with republics and democracies. But I simply want to focus on the money. **This very thing always happens when the money stops flowing**. The French Revolution wasn't unique or profound; it was nothing more than the people rising up and attacking what they thought caused their poverty. Over 17,000 people were tried and executed, and an unknown number of people died in prison without a trial. This was a real revolution by the people. Unfortunately, the crowd mentality is usually wrong. It's my opinion that American slave produced goods, and poor tax policy, set the stage for the French Revolution.

THE CANON OF RECIPROCITY

On Inflation and Deflation

It is technically incorrect of me to clarify what inflation and deflation is this late in the book. It is logical to clearly define terms first and build upon the findings and assertions. I don't mean to patronize you if you already understand what these things mean and how they happen. But I do apologize to those who expect a rigorous, proof-type writing. I started off with the sensational "driverless cars will destroy the country." It feels backwards to start with the combination of possibilities, but I also want the reader to be entertained. Let's first give the definitions of inflation and deflation.

Inflation is a sustained increase in the general price level of goods and services in an economy over a period of time.

Deflation is the sustained decrease in the general price level of goods and services in an economy over a period of time.

Q: What are the causes of inflation/deflation?

A: There are a number of causes for inflation and deflation. There are three factors, pertinent to us, which cause inflation and deflation to occur in a local economy: change in amount of currency, lending, and financial reciprocity. The simplest and most apparent cause is the amount of physical currency in circulation. The US currently uses a Fiat currency; meaning, the dollar isn't backed by some tangible good, i.e., weight in gold. The US Treasury is constantly printing and destroying dollars.

If the Treasury decides to print more dollars than it destroys, and disperses those dollars to the public, something happens. If the supply of dollars are significantly increased and the supply of goods and services don't increase in a commensurate manner, then the prices of goods and services must go up, if and only if the people who received the influx of cash spend the money.

Conversely, if the Treasury decides to decrease the amount of currency available, the opposite will happen. If the supply of money decreases, and the supply of goods and services don't decrease in a commensurate way, then demand must wane for goods and services and prices will drop. The next two will take some explaining.

Money lending can at times seem complex and scary. I think maybe that's what financial institutions want you to think. I believe that banking will radically shift in the coming years. But on to inflation/deflation. Let's consider some basic lending.

Q: I loaned my friend Billy $100, and he promised to pay me back $110, in 30 days. Billy delivered on his promise. Was $10 created?

A: No. Simple lending like this doesn't create inflation or additional currency. Technically speaking, what happened was that part of the flow of wealth, passing through Billy, was directed towards me. Nothing was created or destroyed. It is nothing more than a redirection of wealth.

Q: You said lending causes Inflation! If the loan to Billy didn't cause inflation, then how does lending cause inflation?

A: You are sharp. There was a time in the past where all currency was backed by a precious metal. Banks became a necessity as people couldn't carry around thousands of pounds of gold. A person would deposit their gold or silver into a bank and they would get a note showing they had "X" amount of gold or silver on deposit with said bank. The bank in turn promised to pay the depositor interest based on the length of time the gold or silver was left in the bank.

Once the bank had the deposit of gold/silver, and had a promised rate of return to the depositor, the bank then loaned that gold out to people whom the bank deemed worthy. The interest rate for the borrower would be higher than the interest rate for the depositor. This way the bank would be able to pocket the difference.

Before you ask, there is some inflation, given such an example. If a bank loans out money in this way, what they are mainly doing is redirecting the flow of wealth into their direction and depending on the difference of the interest rates, the rate of change of the flow of wealth. But if a promissory note is given for the same amount of gold, to two different individuals, then the bank in effect has doubled the amount of gold.

Here's where it gets interesting. The gold never left the bank. The bank issued the depositor and the borrower a promissory note for the same gold. Banks realized, at some point, that they could loan the same gold out to multiple people simply by issuing multiple promissory notes.

This is how inflation is created by lending. For example, if a bank receives a pound of gold on deposit, they could then turn around and loan out five pounds of gold. If anyone wanted to see the gold, they could go to the bank and find that their pound of gold is safe and sound. In this example, there are now an extra five pounds of gold in the world. The bank in effect created a lot of currency. Given that they increased the amount of currency, the same rules that we stated earlier apply. The price of goods and services must then go up.

Q: What happens when people start to withdraw their deposits from a bank?

A: The exact opposite happens. Even with only one borrower and one depositor, the situation is dire. If the depositor goes to the bank and withdraws his one pound of gold, then the bank will have no gold on deposit. In order to stay liquid, they will need to go to the only borrower and demand payment. If they succeed in getting back the pound of gold they lent out, then all is right in the world, right? In this simple example, there was effectively a promissory note for two pounds of gold with the bank. One pound of gold evaporated.

It gets worse if the bank loaned the gold out to multiple borrowers. If the depositor withdraws his pound of gold, then the bank may demand payment from one or all of the five borrowers. Meaning, one to five pounds of gold will no longer exist. The amount of available currency will decrease and consequently, the price of goods and services will decrease as a result; this is deflation.

This is the primary reason why we no longer back our currency with gold. Simple banking could potentially cause a catastrophic deflationary event. Now we have a myriad of rules governing banking to ensure that another (and there have been many) catastrophic deflationary event doesn't happen. I know the question that you are asking yourself right now.

Q: How much of my money are banks allowed to lend to others?

A: Fascinating question! Before the financial crisis of 2008, banks were allowed to have a leverage ratio of 3%. By 2014, the leverage ratio was upped to a whopping 5%!

Q: What is a leverage ratio?

A: The leverage ratio is the assets to capital on a bank's balance sheet.

Q: I'm confused. Please use simple language; what does this mean?

A: Banks are now suffering under tough new restrictions from our government. They are now only allowed 20:1 leverage. So to put it simply, if you put $1 in your local bank, then they in turn loan that dollar out twenty times. Seems fair, no? They are currently fighting tooth and nail to lower those requirements.

Q: I understand how printing more money and lending causes inflation and deflation, but what is this reciprocity nonsense?

A: The multiplicative effect of reciprocity is vital and pertinent in our economy. First, because it has an effect on the supply of currency. Secondly, because no one seems to be paying attention to it. We've already discussed how money itself multiplies with reciprocity. But we didn't look at it in terms of inflation and deflation.

"Natural" inflation happens when there are reciprocal financial relationships. I myself call it natural. It's natural because there doesn't need to be a complicated algorithm to create it. It simply happens when people, businesses, or governments buy and sell things.

Q: Reciprocity doesn't make sense. If the government has $X in revenue and spends $Y, how can $Y spending yield dollars greater then $X without raising taxes?

A: I think the hardest thing to grasp is the economic effect of spending. Each node, small or large, should be thought of as way stations for wealth. Or, to make a good analogy, let's use ball bearings. Each ball bearing has its own unique rotation, directionality, force, and size. If you pass a dollar over one of the ball bearings, something happens. The dollar will be directed in a direction with a certain speed. Larger ball bearings are able to direct larger amounts of dollars.

If we are to think about reciprocity as ball bearings, there is a question of whether or not a dollar returns to an individual ball bearing after it has left. It would be vital to know how many ball bearings touched that dollar and how long it took to return to the first ball bearing. If the dollar did return to the original ball bearing, then that dollar had an economic effect of $1 for every ball bearing it touched.

Life would be simple if every node were a ball bearing. It becomes complicated when a percentage of every dollar goes towards taxes. Then it gets even hairier when you consider that some nodes are huge and do nothing but redirect wealth and not spend it. If we assume that everyone is nice and spends money equally and with commensurate reciprocity, then it makes sense that the government can in fact increase its reserves with reciprocity.

As each node is fluid, if the government spends $1, and all the nodes have high reciprocity, that dollar could have an economic effect of $10 on the local economy. If the government receives 20% in taxes, then it gets $2 in tax revenue. The same rules apply when additional dollars are created — you get inflation.

This is if and only if there is financial reciprocity. If even a single node is uncooperative, it would have a deflationary effect on the economy, which is what we have now and which would be considered deflation. If given our same example of a single dollar having an economic effect of ten dollars, and one of the initial people simply pockets the dollar, then there would be a decrease in dollars in the economy. If it was the first person, then he removed $9 from the local economy. This decrease in currency will ultimately lead to deflation.

Who is Right, Dems or Pubs?

It is fascinating to watch our political process. It appears that both parties have officially adopted inflationary or deflationary policies. Then both attempt to look to examples from the past when inflationary or deflationary policies were correct. First, let's ask the question.

Q: Which is better, inflation or deflation?

A: It is a common understanding that government officials aim for about a 3% annual inflation rate. Their reasoning is simple: "It keeps the money flowing." With a constant inflation rate, people can't hoard their money as they will be losing 3% of the value of the money every year. Given a steady 3% per year increase, home prices will rise, and supposedly wages as well. This 3% is supposed to maintain a healthy flow of wealth. By the way, it never happens. There is almost never a healthy flow of wealth.

Which is better? In my opinion, neither. I don't believe we should be aiming for inflation or deflation. We should be aiming directly for a healthy flow of wealth. Both inflationary and deflationary policies will be necessary for creating a healthy flow.

What's interesting about the inflation versus deflation arguments, is that most people agree on doing inflationary policies, which is a reflection of our current political stances. Inflationary policies reflect a majority of the people and deflationary policies reflect a minority. But the minority has most of the money.

Q: I thought you were a Democrat! How can you not want inflationary policies?

A: I'll repeat again: I'm sure that I'm a conservative. But I can't stand all the racism in the Republican Party. I'm also not saying that inflation is bad or good. It just is. The problem with inflation and deflation is that people only remember the drastic changes. Everyone remembers the glorious days when inflation was rampant. Prices were going up, everyone was getting raises, and home values were through the roof! Why would anyone not want more of that? When it comes to deflation, people remember falling prices in goods and services, they remember all of the job losses, and they remember the value of their homes dropping.

The problem with current inflationary or deflationary policies is that they don't account for the flow of wealth or financial reciprocity. If wealth is exchanging hands too much, or there is too much inflation in any capacity, deflationary policies are necessary. Also, if wealth isn't exchanging hands locally, or there is too much deflation, then inflationary policies are necessary.

This is how the government tackles local economic conditions. Unfortunately, they don't account for directionality of the wealth, which creates what I call areas of relative inflation/deflation. Economists call such a thing "stagflation."

Stagflation: *is a situation where the inflation rate is high, the economic growth rate slows down, and unemployment remains steadily high.*

There are areas all around the world that experience relative inflation or deflation. Increased government spending will effectively inflate prices for goods and services where that money is directed, but depending on the directionality of the nodes receiving the money, the policy would potentially be made ineffective. It actually might make some people even poorer. There are places all around the world where, no matter how much money is spent there, the people will not only remain poor, but potentially become even poorer. The problem that no one seems to care about is reciprocity.

This is evident with the construction of new arenas, tropical resorts, and even stimulus spending. When a local economy has a negative reciprocity with its neighboring economies, there is no amount of money that will make that local economy healthy. The wealth simply flows out of the community, never to return.

The country can cheer their great achievements in the "good" community, but always seems to brush under the rug places that are left out as an anomaly. If most of the wealth is flowing into one local economy and out of another, then there will be both inflation and deflation. The people in the "bad" community will never be able to afford to enter the "good" community as prices are going up. The people in the "good" community don't want to spend their money in the "bad" community because the prices are going down.

This understanding of reciprocity and relative inflation and deflation leads us to specific corollaries that are as inescapable as the air we breathe. First, **when the relative deflation of specific areas in a local economy becomes large enough, there is at the very least an economic collapse**.

Q: How can relative deflation cause a collapse?

A: If we assume that the government isn't drastically changing the amount of currency in the economy, and we allow for the 20:1 inflation of banks, then it is only a matter of enough people not being able to pay the notes given to them by the banks. So if enough money is flowing out of one location, and never returning, then the wealth in that location is effectively divided. When the wealth is divided enough, people will either lose their jobs or be paid less. This in turn will lead to an inability to pay loans from the banks. When enough people default on their loans, it will set off a cascading effect of catastrophic deflation in all areas. No one will be spared.

The next corollary that follows logically from this is, **economic collapses are rarely contained in one location.** They spread like wildfire all across the globe. We have looked at some examples of this already and will see further examples of this soon.

Economic collapses sometimes breed bloody revolutions, genocides, and civil wars. Once people are unable to take care of their families, things get messy. The final corollary that happens without fail, is that **angry people look to existing divides among the people as the cause of their problems, and they are usually wrong about that.**

The Inevitable Doom of Greenwood

It is incredibly fortunate for us all that the Tulsa Race Riot happened. No, it isn't fortunate that over ten thousand people were left homeless, and that 3K people died. I am absolutely against the violence that happened there. But it is fortunate for us to see what could happen when people were forced to only spend money within their immediate community. Greenwood challenged hundreds of years' worth of propaganda against people of color. The white people in Oklahoma were jealous and didn't understand what made Greenwood so special. So they destroyed the place at the height of its glory. No one was ever able to revive Greenwood for the same reason that it was doomed to failure. Reciprocity.

I don't know where people get the idea that every dollar spent in Greenwood had the economic impact of $100. If that were true, then the entire economy was based on incredibly high inflation. The idea of such radical inflation is terrifying. I understand how it can be that dollars never left the city. Greenwood was beset on all sides with violence towards them. Blacks couldn't shop or live anywhere else.

But back to $100 in economic activity for every $1 spent. This would be a nightmare to maintain. What happens when one person decided to pack up and move someplace else? This person had $1000 to his name. We all would tell him, good for you for making that brave change. But do you see that he would be leaving with $100,000 of Greenwood's wealth? And that is just one person leaving a wealthy area with a reasonable amount of money!

Do you now see how Greenwood was doomed? The violent and brutal racism of the time forced former slaves to create a local economy that naturally multiplied the wealth. Thankfully, we can remember Greenwood for the economic powerhouse that it was. If the whites of the era had decided to leave Greenwood as it was, opportunists would've eventually collapsed the local economy and the entire incident would be nothing more than proof the blacks can't do anything right. It is indeed fortunate for us all that we are able to glimpse into what is possible. The destruction of that town allows me to ask the world, **"How was it possible that recently freed slaves became wealthy, while the rest of the nation remained poor? And how can we recreate that in our country now?"**

The Giant Federal Node

There is currently a vigorous fight in the US about the "size" of the government. This is a battle that has raged since long before the civil war. This is something that we will look at next. I personally don't care for either of the arguments. Republican arguments are a combination of laissez-faire capitalism and the racist compulsion to put down minority groups and women. Democrat arguments center on the redistribution of wealth. No matter how both sides attempt to polish their own turds, they are still stinking turds.

I like to think of the Federal Government as simply a giant node in a sea of smaller nodes. The Federal Government directs wealth, of varying amounts and varying speeds, all throughout the nation. Looking at it as simply a node that has an effect on the local economy yields surprising results.

Let's look at what happens every time the marginal tax rates for the top income earners were reduced. Why the top income earners? Almost all of the nation's wealth passes through the hands of

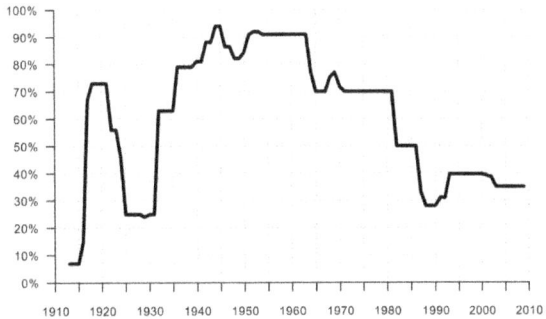

a handful of individuals and corporations. In fact, it has been like this since this nation's inception. Look at the following graph. Here we can clearly see when the rates were raised and dropped.

We can see that progressive taxes started in 1913. This was in response to the monopolies that flourished during this time. Voter anger about income inequality eventually led to a tax rate above 75% for top income earners.

A few years later, when voter anger calmed, the rich were able to significantly lower the top tax rates by 1926. Did that affect the local economy? In October 1929, there was the famous Wall Street crash that ultimately led to the Great Depression. After 1930, the top income tax rate shot to about 90%.

Taxes for top earners remained incredibly high for decades, until 1962 when the rates were poised to drop significantly. Did anything happen? There was a stock market crash in 1962 called the Kennedy Slide, or the Flash Crash of 1962.

The top tax bracket remained the same until 1980, when it was dropped significantly again. Apparently, nothing happened. I believe a collapse didn't happen because of women...Yeah, we'll get to that later. Then rates were significantly dropped again in 1985. The rates went from 70% to less than 30%. In October of 1987, the global collapse known as Black Monday took place.

Finally, in 2003, the top tax bracket was dropped again. In 2008, the US economy suffered a major economic collapse. From which we are still currently recovering.

There are, of course, other extenuating circumstances, considering that we are a part of a global economy. I'm confused that no one has ever pieced together that every major economic crash in the country in the last 100 years coincided with a drop in rates for the top tax bracket.

Q: I thought you weren't for higher taxes! This is liberal propaganda trying to demonize the "job creators!" Do you think taxes should be lowered or not?

A: The taxes are too high and unfair. I'm not for or against either Democratic or Republican policies. I think they both are outdated and won't help our economy. As for attempting to demonize the "job creators," I'm simply pointing out the obvious: The government is nothing more than a giant node where large sums of money exchange hands.

Everyone has their theories about why an economic crash happens. They attempt to point to mistakes of individuals or companies. It's as if the flow of wealth never occurred to anyone. The same thing happens every time you reduce the flow of wealth through any node, small or large; you create a deflationary event. It is unavoidable. Cutting taxes and cutting the expenses of the federal node must create a large deflationary event.

Q: Listen, jerk! Are you for taxes or against taxes? Pick a side!!

A: I'm not for or against taxes. They are nothing more than tools to be used to maintain a healthy flow of wealth. The people who are hell bent on cutting taxes do so for ideology or personal gain. This is a terrible reason for lowering taxes. Without paying attention to the flow of wealth, it could lead to a catastrophic deflationary event.

Making the Case for Small Government

I absolutely believe that the government is too big and taxes are too high. The crashes that I spoke of are indicative of why I believe this. The main problem is that a stable economy needs there to be multiple economic connections between all of the nodes.

Q: What are the best economic connections between the nodes?

A: For true economic stability, the best economic connections are between the smallest nodes. So the Federal Government is the largest, next are State nodes, then City nodes, then Corporate nodes, followed by small business nodes, and finally the nodes of individuals.

Our economy will be the strongest if and only if there are multiple economic connections between individual nodes. The next best are economic connections between small business nodes and individuals, and this continues all the way to the top.

Because cutting taxes on the rich has caused catastrophic deflationary events, doesn't mean that we should never do that. What it means is that our local economy is incredibly anemic and bordering on collapse. It's interesting to note that our current economy seems to be somewhat ok with relatively low tax rates. The current tax rate would not have been effective in 1913. This is because over the last 100 years, many of the individual nodes have dramatically changed. More on that later.

Q: Should the government handle tasks itself or should the private sector handle the majority of the tasks?

A: Given my premise, it honestly doesn't matter if the private sector handling the government tasks has an equal or better reciprocity rate than the government. I think at the heart of the debate over public versus private is the bitter hatred of unions by the one percenters. The thing is, if companies were financially responsible in the communities that they operate in, then there would not be a need for any unions.

Q: What financial role should the federal node play in the economy?

A: The Federal Government should provide essential services that benefit all people in the country; e.g., roads, bridges, health care, power infrastructure, defense, sanitation, mail, and so on. I would be hesitant to hand any of these things over to the private sector unless it made financial sense for the public. Also, the Federal Government should sponsor research that is simply too expensive for individuals or companies to afford and that benefits all the people; e.g., the internet.

What I'm against are subsidies and government loans. These things are the government's efforts at shaping the economic future of the nation. Unfortunately, the federal node is far too large for these things. These things create imbalances that could lead to a deflationary event. Student loans, FHA loans, farm subsidies, and oil subsidies are prime examples of this. FHA loans were at the heart of the 2008 financial crisis. There is currently a student loan bubble ready to pop. According to the New York Federal Reserve, delinquency on student loan rates is currently higher than any other delinquency in the nation. The government is simply too big to be involved with small things and specific industries. It must create an imbalance.

The federal node has the power to, and should, create and foster an environment of healthy financial reciprocity. Apart from the giant things that only the Federal Government can handle, the focus should be on tracking the flow of wealth. A smaller, more nimble government would be preferable. In addition, the taxes needn't be as high if there is enough reciprocity. In fact, if the taxes remain as they are, the inflation of good reciprocity could get out of hand.

REVOLUTION: THE FAILURE OF THE FREE MARKET

From the Ashes of Catastrophic Deflation Arises a Leader

"History is the version of past events that people have decided to agree upon." Napoleon Bonaparte

When we last left our fledgling US, they apparently had won the freedom to trade as they wished and with whom they wished. As good fortune would have it, there was turmoil in Europe. The bloody French Revolution spilled all throughout the region. War meant profits for the world's factory, the United States. While it would be nice to only focus on the United States, events unfolding in Europe would lead America onto a different path than it originally wanted.

Napoleon Bonaparte was affiliated with Augustin Robespierre, brother of Maximilien Robespierre, the leader of the French Revolution. Napoleon rose in military rank quickly during the bloody Reign of Terror, which killed over 17,000 people. Both Robespierres were executed in 1794 and Napoleon was put under house arrest for associating himself with the brothers.

Napoleon's house arrest didn't last long. In 1795, there was a royalist insurrection, in France, and the revolutionary government requested Napoleon's military expertise be put to use for the revolution that he helped create.

Before we continue, I'd like to reiterate what has transpired by following the money. There was extreme poverty in France due to a poor tax structure and large bank debts due to war, and the country subsisted on slave produced goods from America. All of these things redirected the flow of wealth away from certain areas in France and created pockets of relative deflation. The people ultimately revolted against what they believed was the cause of their problems: royalty. In 1795, the

Revolutionary Army crushed the royal opposition in France. Then they went on a global campaign attacking royalty.

Royalty all throughout Europe saw the French Revolution as a threat, joined together, and fought in the War of First Coalition. The coalition consisted of Spain, Holland, Austria, Prussia, England, and Sardinia. The war of the First Coalition lasted from 1792 through 1797. The French Revolutionary government was beset on all sides. First with internal strife with royalists and secondly with the surrounding Royal Empires that wanted to crush a bloody revolution against royalty in its infancy.

In 1793, the French instituted a draft and counterattacked, led by Napoleon. The French were able to repel the First Coalition and defeat the internal insurrections. The French signed treaties with various empires, and gained new land from victory, but France still had plans to annihilate royalty.

The War of the Second Coalition, from 1798 to 1802, included Britain, Austria, Russia, the Ottoman Empire, Portugal, and Naples. These monarchies again attempted to contain the French Revolution. In the midst of constant war, Napoleon initiated a coup and became the leader of the Revolutionary government. The military prowess of Napoleon again proved to be too much for the Royal Coalition. The war ended with more treaties.

The War of the Third Coalition, from 1803 to 1806, involved Britain, Austria, Russia, Sweden, and the Holy Roman Empire (Germany.) This coalition too led to a resounding defeat by Napoleon's military genius. France gained more territories and further treaties were signed.

The War of the Fourth Coalition, 1806-1807, included Britain, Russia, Austria, Prussia, Saxony, and Sweden. This coalition was again defeated by Napoleon. Again land was lost and treaties were signed. It seemed as if Napoleon could do nothing but win. The French aggression continued all throughout Europe. The Revolution was supposed to be the end of royalty, but by this time Napoleon had crowned himself emperor.

The War of the Fifth Coalition, in 1809, included Britain, Austria, Portugal, and Spain. Napoleon invaded nation after nation and installed republics in the place of royalty. The fifth war ended again with a treaty and further land acquisitions for France.

The War of the Sixth Coalition was between 1812 and 1814, and included Russia, Prussia, Austria, and Britain. This is where the tide turned for the French Revolution. All lands seized by France were returned to their respective countries or empires. Further treaties were signed and Napoleon was exiled.

The War of the Seventh Coalition, the Hundred Days, in 1815, included Britain, Russia, Prussia, and Austria. This happened after Napoleon escaped exile and resumed power in France. Napoleon's military campaigns ended with the famous Battle of Waterloo. He lost and was exiled again, where he remained until death.

People look at Napoleon Bonaparte as an anomaly in history. It is fortunate for the French people that they did have such a capable and charismatic leader. He was a military genius, but Napoleon is by no means unique. Quite often, in times of catastrophic deflation, an intelligent, charismatic leader emerges and wages a war against what he believes is the cause of the people's suffering. **His ability to sway the people is proportional to the economic suffering those people suffered.**

The Other Little Man

It was well known that Napoleon was a man of diminutive stature. Across the pond, around the time of Napoleon's reign, was another small man with a great mind: James Madison. Madison was 5 foot 4 inches and weighed about one hundred pounds. He is considered one of the greatest minds of the Revolution. He personally drafted the first ten amendments to the Constitution. Madison was Secretary of State to Thomas Jefferson, and right after became the President in 1809.

America had a treaty with both Britain and France, but as the international campaigns against France mounted, American trade was affected. Both Britain and France imposed trade restrictions with America, in order to weaken the other's economy. America attempted to remain neutral in order to keep trading with both. In time, Britain simply blockaded the entire American coastline.

The blockade stifled the American profit engine. In addition to blocking trade, Britain seized American goods, and impressed Americans to fight for them. Impressment was the act of kidnapping Americans and forcing them to fight in the war against France. In case there was any confusion about how the British felt about forced labor, look no further than the impressment of American sailors. I don't believe the stirring rebuke from the Supreme Court Justice about American slavery had anything to do with moral objections. If so, what's the difference between capturing Africans and forcing them to work, and capturing Americans and forcing them to fight?

In 1807, Thomas Jefferson tried to peacefully end the hostilities toward America with the Embargo Act. This act made any and all exports, from the US, illegal. It was intended to hurt both Britain and France. Unfortunately, Britain simply got its goods from other colonies in the Americas, and also the American traders simply ignored the ban. It had only been a few years since its inception, but the US was ungovernable even for the US. The United States were a loose collaboration of disparate business interests, all believing in the wonders of the "free market."

As Jefferson left office, in 1809, the Embargo Act was repealed. The idea that the US was an actual country was laughable. Its citizens were being kidnapped and forced to fight in a foreign war and its goods were being seized. Most of the country just wanted the money to continue to flow, and to each his own.

Before Madison had become president, he was a strong proponent of "State's Rights" over the Federal Government. He was also strongly opposed to a national bank. As a slave plantation owner from Virginia, those positions made sense. Governing these ideas was a particular challenge for Madison. Before Madison was President, wars raged continuously in Europe and challenged his own ideology.

Madison, after becoming President, was stuck with a monumental task. The British blockade and impressment was a slap in the face of the US. The people showed no unity when it came to the suffering of its fellow citizens. The only thing that mattered was continued profit. Madison realized that there were many unresolved issues stemming from the American Revolution. The only reason Americans had their independence was due to French involvement. What would happen if France lost the war against Britain? The US was no military threat to the British Empire and the great disrespect of forcing slavery upon its citizen's was proof of what the Empire thought of the US.

This was the first true test of the Constitution that Madison helped write. Madison was one of the main proponents of the separation of powers in the Constitution. He went to Congress and asked them to declare war on the British Empire. In 1812, after years of vigorous debate, the Congress voted in favor of war. Forty percent of the

Congress, in both houses, voted no on the war. This war was unpopular from the beginning. It made trade more difficult with Britain, and was seen as unwinnable, since the US had almost no soldiers.

If you contrast the reality of the War of 1812, and the glorious retelling of the American Revolution, you'd see that something is off just a bit. America revolted against the most powerful empire on the planet because the taxes on imports were too onerous? Only a few years later, there were violent protests against the War of 1812, when the British Empire was literally stealing citizens and goods. There was so little unity in the nation that this war was affectionately known as "James' War." In my opinion, impressment is far more outrageous than taxes on foreign molasses.

For two years, the "war" raged, but for the British Empire, known as the United Kingdom by then, the War of 1812 was a nonevent. Once Napoleon abdicated in 1814, the UK sent seasoned reinforcements to the US. The War of 1812 was nothing but defeat after defeat for the US. After the end of the wars in Europe, the UK armed forces simply marched through America and torched what was then the White House. Madison was the only president who had to flee the presidential mansion for safety reasons.

Even though the UK was clearly a superior force, the fact that Madison didn't surrender helped this nation survive. The UK was hurting financially from years of battle. History books say that there was an impasse, but I think the UK realized how ungovernable the US was and made a financial decision to end the fighting. Also, I believe they had other ways to attack the US.

I believe this was the real American Revolution. Without any other nation's help, America defied the might of the United Kingdom and survived. The resilience of Madison is what shaped what we are today. In fact, the experience of the War of 1812 shifted Madison's opinions, which changed our destiny as well.

Slavery – The Divisive Issue

A lot transpired in the US between the War of 1812 and the Civil War in 1861. Looking at the events as they unfold may not be best suited for our purposes. The main reason I'd like to take a step back is the conflicting "histories" surrounding these events. Some say the Civil War was fought in order to stop slavery, and others say it was to uphold the Constitution. There are variants to both sides of this debate. This is what makes history such a tricky subject. The prevailing historical narrative is written by the victors. I'd like to clarify my position right now: I disagree.

Slavery itself was at the heart of the debate, but improving the lives of the slaves was not. The entire nation was and still is steeped in the belief of white male supremacy. You may not wish to agree with me out loud, but white male supremacy is simply the belief that some people are born better than others. Whites are born better than blacks, and men are born better than women. This idea of white male supremacy was never really addressed. If that is so, what was the Civil War fought over?

There are many causes of the Civil War, and I will attempt to share each of them with you. The main issue of the Civil War was in fact political power. Before the War of 1812, the Federal Government was weak and ineffectual, as the founders had intended. There was a clear balance of power among the states in the Federal Legislature. From the very beginning of our nation, we had to deal with the humanity of the slaves. The number of representatives in the House of Representatives was to be determined by population. Also, electoral votes for the president were decided by population. The Southern states, who had large slave populations, wanted the slaves to be counted as people, thus giving them a significant majority in the House. This majority would last for ten years, as this was the interval the census was to be taken. The Northern states opposed the slaves being counted as they would be in a political minority. The 3/5s Compromise was adopted to maintain the balance of power. Slaves were counted as three-fifths of a person during each census.

From the very beginning, the political divide in our country was between people with slaves and people without slaves, each side jockeying for a political edge over the other. While I do believe that there were people who did morally object to the treatment of the slaves, the crux of the matter was political power.

After the Louisiana Purchase of 1803, Congress was compelled to establish a policy regarding the expansion of slavery. More pro-slavery states would outnumber the anti-slavery proponents in the House and the Senate. When Missouri applied to be a state, there was a bitter national debate. Missouri wanted to be a pro-slavery state, and accepting it into the Union would tip the balance of power. In 1820, the Missouri Compromise was reached. Missouri was accepted into the Union, but a new state, Maine, was created to maintain the balance of power. Maine was created by dividing Massachusetts. Also, all new states below the 36'30 parallel would be slave states and all above would be free states.

In 1846, David Wilmot introduced a bill called the Wilmot Proviso. It was a bill to outlaw the expansion of slavery into lands acquired by the US as a result of war. The Proviso never passed due to bitter opposition by the slave holding states. Again, this was a political struggle to see who would control the government. If the slave states allowed this Proviso, then slavery would be banned in states from the Southwest all the way to California.

In 1850, the Congress brokered the Compromise of 1850. This compromise prevented further expansion of slavery and strengthened the Fugitive Slave Act, a law that compelled Northern states to seize and return escaped slaves to the South. While this seems like an intense nationwide political battle, it was in fact nothing more than a battle between the political powers of rich white men. It wasn't until 1856 that all white men were given the right to vote, regardless of property ownership. The Fugitive Slave Act itself opened up the eyes of average Americans to the horrors of American slavery. It made Northerners complicit in the barbarity of slavery.

In 1857, the Supreme Court ruled in the case Dred Scott versus Sanford. Dred Scott was a Virginia slave who sued for his freedom. The Court ruled that Scott was a piece of property and had no legal rights or recognitions as a human being. Chief Justice Roger Taney famously proclaimed that blacks are "so far inferior that they had no rights which the white man was bound to respect."[4] This case was incredibly significant as it essentially made slavery the law of the entire land. The Supreme Court itself interjected into the controversial topic of slavery, and essentially decreed that anti-slavery states had no standing, thus calling into question every political compromise made. This emboldened the pro-slavery activists to expand slavery into places where they were barred, thus upsetting the balance of power.

This is just the beginning of the challenges facing the country, that

---

[4]   Library of Congress

led to the Civil War. It is important to lay the political framework that caused the schism. There was a power struggle between wealthy white men, which centered on slavery, not white supremacy. This political struggle was fought in each branch of government.

As with the case of most activist Supreme Courts, the people tend to vote in the opposite direction. Abraham Lincoln was elected as President, by a considerable margin, in 1860, despite not even being on the ballot in many Southern States. Abraham Lincoln's election struck fear into the hearts of Southerners. In 1860, a month after the polls closed, South Carolina seceded from the Union. Six more states followed South Carolina by the spring of 1861.

Technology Destroyed American Slavery

Growing up, I was taught when and where slavery ended. We had to memorize dates and countries. I was told again and again that, "Slavery built this nation." I do remember asking once, "If slavery was such a good thing, why did it stop?" My tiny white American History teacher adjusted his nerd glasses and said, "People all around the world stood up and fought against this deplorable practice. One nation after the other outlawed it because it has no place in modern society." We debated for a short while, because he didn't answer the question. If slavery itself brought massive profits to America, then it should have never ended.

The reality is, slavery was never and still isn't a financial boon to anyone, except the slave owners. American style slavery was in fact doomed by technology. As technology rapidly advanced, it made a large force of forced, uneducated, manual labor obsolete.

The slave states all seemed to uniformly adopt cotton as their cash crop. This was for a number of reasons. The first and most obvious was that cotton didn't rot or spoil. The plantations could store up as much cotton as they wanted and sell when they pleased. Cotton was in high demand as it was used in all types of cloth and clothing. Cotton could be shipped overseas or to the textile factories in New York for production. Next, cotton was labor intensive. First cotton was handpicked, then the seeds needed to be removed from the cotton. America had a competitive advantage in cotton due to its massive slave force.

The first nail in the coffin for slavery was the cotton gin. In 1794, Eli Whitney's simple cotton gin was able to do the work of dozens of slaves. It was able to quickly remove the seeds from the cotton mechanically. In the beginning, this machine was powered by horses. There was still a need for people to pick the cotton.

The biggest threat to American slavery was the steam engine. In 1781, James Watt patented a steam engine that produced a continuous rotary motion. This engine was measured by the power of a single horse. Watt's first engine had the power of ten horses. Adding the steam engine to the cotton gin further made slaves less useful.

You may think that this isn't such a big deal, but consider the global implications of just these two inventions. It made it possible for people all around the world to compete with America's giant slave force. By the way, the slaves themselves worked for free, but it wasn't free. The slaves needed to be housed, fed, and aggressively watched and abused. All of these things cost money. With every technological advance, American slavery slowly lost its competitive edge.

You would think that slaveholding states would have an edge in the House, given that they could simply buy more slaves or force the slaves to breed. More unskilled workers wouldn't mean more money. Technology itself forced the slaveholding states to cut back on expanding their slave population, thus putting them in a tenuous political position.

The steam engine did far more damage to slave states than just make their labor force a little obsolete. In 1833, the steamship, The Great Western, crossed the Atlantic Ocean in 15 days. Before the steamship, it took three months to cross the Atlantic Ocean. Poor Europeans simply couldn't afford to make the trip on their own. Thus, they needed to indenture themselves to those who would sponsor their three month voyage. It's not clear to me when the practice of indentured servitude ended. But by the 1860s, it took eight days to cross the Atlantic Ocean by steamship. It suddenly became financially practical for even the poorest of people to buy a one way ticket on a packed ship, headed to America.

Slave states had a demographics problem. Europeans would land in New York and stay mostly in the Northern states. This was mainly due to the fact that it was difficult to compete with slave labor. The available work of the time was in textiles. The only work to be had was in non-slave states. Work in America was difficult and the people were mostly poor. Some did go back to their home countries, but most stayed as Europe was suffering severe financial issues. If nothing drastic was done, by 1860 the new census may have tipped the demographic scale in favor of the non-slave states.

These two technological advances were more than enough to stifle the American slave system. So many people in this country still opine the good ole days. If only the South had won its independence things would be different, right? By 1944, the mechanical cotton picker became viable. If by some miracle the South seceded successfully, the entire slave economy would've begun to collapse upon itself in 1944.

Political Activism – The Bane of Slavery

While I don't believe that the abolition of slavery itself was at the heart of the Civil War, the act of slavery produced a number of unintended consequences. At this time there were about four million slaves in the US. Most of the slaves resided in the South. Slaves running away were incredibly common. There was wide open spaces and jungle all around. Some slaves were willing to risk death by running away. It was a terrifying ordeal for everyone involved. You had hungry and terrified runaways all across the country not knowing who to trust. Any of the whites could kill them or put them back into slavery. If a white person did see an escaped slave in the bushes, his life could be in danger.

Individual slaves running away on their own wasn't a huge problem, as the entire community was on high alert for such a thing. The real problem for slavery was activist abolitionists. They organized themselves into what was called the Underground Railroad. But what most people don't realize is that these very abolitionists were active at the inception of our country. In 1786, George Washington wrote a letter to his friend Robert Morris, complaining that a slave had escaped from one of his neighbors and that, "A society of Quakers, formed for such purposes, have attempted to liberate him...acting repugnant to justice...[and], in my opinion, extremely impoliticly with respect to the State."

Underground Railroad literally means "the secret journey of fleeing slaves to freedom." Safe houses were called "Stations," and the owners of the safe houses were known as "Station Masters." People who gave money or goods were called "Stockholders." The escaped slaves were known as "Goods." The "Conductors" were those who planned the routes and often accompanied the runaway slaves.

The Underground Railroad assisted up to 100,000 runaway slaves. Compared to the four million still in captivity, it seems like a small number. But to the pro-slavery South, the Underground Railroad represented an existential threat. It gave the remaining slaves hope for freedom. American slavery rested on the idea that the slave was nothing more than chattel, a piece of furniture, or like a cow. This belief was ingrained into every aspect of American life. The social order can only be maintained if the chattel themselves believe this immutable fact of the universe.

In 1831, Nat Turner, a slave, incited an uprising that spread through several plantations in Virginia. Turner and around 70 others killed 60 white people. The military ultimately suppressed this uprising. Fifty-five slaves were tried and executed for their role in the revolt. Almost two hundred more slaves were lynched by mobs. The Southern states had much to fear. There were frequent slave uprisings. They were common and small scale. Nat Turner changed the calculus dramatically.

Harriet Beecher Stowe, an abolitionist, fought slavery in her own way. Her book, *Uncle Tom's Cabin*, was a fictional exploration of slave life. This book was second only to the Bible in the bestselling books of the nineteenth century. Northerners felt as if their eyes were opened to

the horrific reality of slavery. Southerners said that Stowe's book was slanderous.

In 1854, after bitter arguing, brandishing weapons, and death threats, Congress overturned parts of the Missouri Compromise by allowing settlers in Kansas and Nebraska to vote on whether to allow slavery in their respective states. Pro-slavery and anti-slavery activists flocked to Kansas in order to affect the vote. For five years, the two sides fought physically. During this time, fifty-six people died because of the conflict, and it was thus named "Bleeding Kansas." Both became slave free states.

One of the anti-slavery leaders in the Bleeding Kansas event was John Brown. He was a religious zealot, murderer, crusading abolitionist, revolutionary, and anything else you could possibly say. In researching for this book, I was surprised to have never heard about this man. The more I learn, the more I can see why history books leave him out. No one can agree on whether or not he was a good person or not. But for our purposes, he would be a major catalyst in the Civil War.

In 1859, John Brown and a small group raided a government arsenal in Virginia. He hoped to spark a revolution by distributing weapons to the slaves. Unfortunately, the depot was quickly surrounded by militia and eventually by soldiers under the command of Robert E. Lee. He was tried for treason and became a martyr for the abolitionist cause. But in the South, after this event, they began to mobilize militarily.

Why would they begin to mobilize? John Brown's raid was organized and financed by the "Secret Six." We now know who the six were: Thomas Wentworth Higginson, Samuel Gridley Howe, Theodore Parker, Franklin Benjamin Sanborn, Gerrit Smith, and George Luther Stearns. It was bad enough that Southerners had to worry about runaway slaves and slave revolts, now they had to be on the lookout for white people as well. A year later, Southern states seceded.

Financial Collapse – Are You Surprised?

By 1857, financial collapses had become commonplace. Banks would fail and people would rush the banks to get their gold out first. Because the world economies had become intertwined, the Panic of 1857 was considered the first worldwide economic crisis. Listing the causes of each crash is somewhat tedious and backward. I'll list the supposed "causes" as this is what history has decided the causes to be. But for my purposes, the cause is and always will be the flow of wealth. If wealth continues to flow in only one direction, there must be an economic crash.

The Panic was supposed to have started in Britain, when government officials circumvented the banking laws requiring that gold and silver reserves back up the amount of money in circulation. When news of this spread, there was a run on the banks "causing" a financial collapse in Britain, which spread throughout the world.

At the same time as the run on the banks in Britain, 30,000 pounds of gold were lost at sea coming from the San Francisco Mint headed to Eastern banks. Four hundred people died when this boat sank. This set off a panic in America as well.

With these rushes on the banks in full swing, the New York branch of the Ohio Life Insurance and Trust Co. collapsed due to massive embezzlement. Are you surprised yet? This further fueled the financial crisis.

When the money stops flowing, people stop spending, and the prices for goods and services plummet: deflation. This caused a significant drop in grain prices, hurting the rural areas. Manufactured goods began to pile up in warehouses, leading to massive layoffs. Land speculation collapsed along with railroad companies and construction. The money simply evaporated.

It's important to note that the South was less hurt by the economic crisis. There was still demand for cotton. Southerners took this news as a sign that their economic system was superior to the North. They were just fortunate.

The deep global financial collapse can't be said to be the main cause of the Civil War. But bloody revolutions, civil wars, genocides, and the like are usually preceded by a catastrophic financial event. The divides that already exist become exacerbated. If the South didn't secede, something else momentous would've likely happened.

The Kernel that Caused the Civil War

There is one main reason why the Civil War was fought: American Exceptionalism. Before I attempt to define this commonly used phrase, let me touch on slavery once more. Slavery was at the heart of the issue as the political fortunes rested on how the population was counted. The South had a major demographics problem, and they still do.

"**American exceptionalism** is a belief that the United States is unique or exceptional when compared with the historical development of other countries."[5] I found this on the web, I suppose it could suffice. For me, American exceptionalism is code for white male supremacy. Even though non-whites and females have accepted this ideology, it still holds true. This belief that you can do anything if you just put effort into it, that seems well and good, until you realize that people who aren't successful are believed to not hold this belief.

In essence, American exceptionalism is defined as a "culture," and if only others possessed this "culture," they too would be like us. It's in our media, the news, and in stories. It's like a never ending propaganda campaign about how great some of us are. I use the term American exceptionalism here so that we all understand what I'm talking about. Back then, it was just plain old white male supremacy.

After the UK withdrew its troops from the US, all was well, right? No. The British didn't give up. They tried a different strategy to overthrow our government. They began to flood the US markets with cheap goods produced in India. Tactically speaking, this was a brilliant move on the part of the British. The Americans went up against the most powerful force on the planet twice, survived, and were arrogant about it. They sang the praises of free trade all throughout the globe. Though James Madison, a slave plantation owner, was vehemently against a national bank, taxes, and a strong Federal Government, being President shifted his own personal beliefs.

In 1787, James Madison addressed the Constitutional Convention in Philadelphia stating, *"A standing military force, with an overgrown Executive will not long be safe companions to liberty... The means of defense against foreign danger, have been always the instruments of tyranny at home. Among the Romans it was a standing maxim to excite a war, whenever a revolt was apprehended. Throughout all Europe, the armies kept up under the pretext of defending, have enslaved the people."*

After the War of 1812, Madison saw the light. He now believed that there needed to be a strong central government with a standing army, to

[5]   http://rationalwiki.org/

enforce the laws of the Federal Government and to defend the people. He favored and promoted the idea of having a strong national banking system. Finally, he proposed a "protective tariff" on imported goods. These things were funded by the Tariff of 1816. This tariff goes against the entire narrative of the American existence. Freshly out of war, the congress ratified this new law. One notable person who voted against the tariff was John Randolph, arguing to congress:

> "It eventuates in this: whether you, as a planter will consent to be taxed, in order to hire another man to go to work in a shoemaker's shop, or to set up a spinning jenny. For my part I will not agree to it, even though they should, by way of return, agree to be taxed to help us to plant tobacco; much less will I agree to pay all, and receive nothing for it. No, I will buy where I can get manufactures cheapest; I will not agree to lay a duty on the cultivators of the soil to encourage exotic manufactures; because, after all, we should only get much worse things at a much higher price, and we, the cultivators of the country, would in the end pay all."

America, after all, stood up to the tyrannical British Empire and their protective tariffs. Why should Americans stand for tariffs coming from the Federal Government? There is, and has been, a fantasy that it was the free market that set America free from England. It was, in fact, the French. There is this fantasy that tariffs versus the free market was at the heart of the American Revolution. It was much more likely that Americans were afraid of losing their slaves. If there is any doubt about whether this is true, there was no revolt in America when the very same tariffs were introduced by the Federal Government.

The American free trade fantasy met reality in 1812. No amount of rolling up of sleeves and getting to work would have saved the American economy from a flood of cheap goods from India. Madison knew this and the UK knew this. I don't think the UK expected that the US would enact such laws; I actually don't believe it myself.

To me, the Federal Government was born in 1816, much to the chagrin of people who believed in "American exceptionalism." With a standing army, the Federal Government could now enact laws and enforce them. This is literally not what the Founders fought for, including Madison. The President was now more powerful than individual governors. The Federal Legislators could do as they wished in the country, thus setting the stage for fierce political battles. If only one could maintain power in the Federal Government, all would be fine.

Tariffs were the main way the Federal Government financed itself. But taxes and a strong central government, with rules and regulations, goes against free market principles. These free market principles were being challenged directly by the UK. Entire industries in the North were being driven out of business by ever cheaper products from India. The Congress then passed the Tariff of 1828 to protect those very industries.

This Tariff was dubbed "Tariff of Abominations" by Southerners. The Tariff itself was a 62% tax on 92% of all imported goods. The British effectively destroyed the nation by playing upon the fantasies of its inception. The South essentially had only one product: cotton. They were dependent on others for all other goods. By flooding the US with cheaply produced goods, the factories in the North were going out of business.

This dilemma brought forth the "American exceptionalism" in Southerners. The Vice President at the time, John C. Calhoun, anonymously wrote in an article entitled "South Carolina Exposition and Protest," stating that, "We [the South] cultivate certain staples for the supply of the general market of the world; and they [the North] manufacture almost exclusively for the home market. Their object in the tariff is to keep down foreign competition, in order to obtain a monopoly of the domestic market…" Calhoun even encouraged the idea of Nullification. Nullification is the belief that states have the right to nullify any federal law which that state declares unconstitutional.

Instead of viewing what was happening to the US as an existential threat from the UK, Southerners accused Northerners of "taking their stuff." Northern states weren't "exceptional." It was their own fault for not being able to compete. To Southerners, this Tariff was a large transfer of wealth from the South to the North. If you look at it microscopically, that may be the case, but there was no way that the US could survive if part of it collapsed due to cheap goods from India. This argument has yet to go away. Entire cities today are desolate due to foreign trade. Even still today, people blame those cities for not being exceptional.

Eventually, the nullification crisis was averted and the Tariff was reduced back to the rates of 1816. Yet the problem still persisted. The

UK was flooding the American markets with cheap goods. The "I got mines, Jack" philosophy still persisted. It would be only a matter of time before a collapse happened. That collapse eventually became the Civil War.

The Real Abe Lincoln

I can't seem to understand why history taught in schools is so wrong. It's quite vexing to know that I was lied to my entire youth. The only thing I can kind of say for sure is that maybe Abe really was honest. If that is the case, then we can let Abraham Lincoln himself explain how he felt about the Negroes.

In 1858, in a debate with Stephen Douglas, for an Illinois US Senate seat, Lincoln said this about "negro equality": "I will say then that I am not, nor ever have been, in favor of bringing about in anyway the social and political equality of the white and black races — that I am not nor ever have been in favor of making voters or jurors of negroes, nor of qualifying them to hold office, nor to intermarry with white people; and I will say in addition to this that there is a physical difference between the white and black races which I believe will forever forbid the two races living together on terms of social and political equality. And inasmuch as they cannot so live, while they do remain together, there must be the position of superior and inferior, and I as much as any other man am in favor of having the superior position assigned to the white race."

Abraham Lincoln did kind of think slavery was wrong. But he was no abolitionist. The abolitionists of that day were similar to the Greenpeace of today. The abolitionists were small in number, but passionate about what they did. It is an offense to the people who actually risked their lives to compare Lincoln with an abolitionist. I've found far too many clearly white supremacist quotes from Lincoln. I don't want to waste too much ink quoting him.

But if there are any doubters as to whether or not the war was fought over slavery, you can trust honest Abe. "My paramount object in this struggle is to save the Union, and is not either to save or to destroy slavery. If I could save the Union without freeing any slave, I would do it, and if I could save it by freeing all the slaves, I would do it; and if

I could save it by freeing some and leaving others alone, I would also do that. What I do about slavery, and the colored race, I do because I believe it helps to save the Union…"[6]

The famed Emancipation Proclamation didn't in fact free all of the slaves. The slaves in states that didn't rebel weren't affected by this proclamation. Slaves in Delaware, Maryland, Kentucky, and Missouri remained slaves as these states were still in the Union. The Emancipation Proclamation was a military tactic. First, they hoped to spark a slave insurrection in the Confederacy, and secondly, escaped slaves were signing up in droves to fight for the Union.

American Fantasies Fail Miserably

I want to reiterate why the South seceded. It's like an Ayn Rand pipe dream. The wealthiest states with the best war generals wished to escape from the losers in the North. They may have stayed if there was a clear path to a majority, in political terms. But the wealthy are always a minority in the free market. With expanded suffrage, the white males in the North would always outnumber the white males in the South. Then, having your own guy in the White House was almost impossible. Next, the flow of immigrants into the North was likely to tip the balance in the house in 1860, a census year. Why should the South financially "support" people who don't know how the world works?

Many people focus on the actual battles in the Civil War, but I'm not going to. Those battles aren't relevant to my purposes. The South did have better generals, and maybe could have won the war. In fact, the internet is rife with people looking over the missteps that could've turned the tide. I disagree entirely. I believe the North saved the South from its disastrous policies. It may have been better for the North to have lost, for us to be done with these nonsensical notions. But they keep coming back generation after generation as if the Confederacy never lost.

The first extreme policy failure came when the South demanded that European nations recognize its legitimacy. They used "Cotton Diplomacy." In a speech before the US Senate, Sen. James Henry

---

[6]   Letter to Horace Greeley, August 22, 1862

Hammond of South Carolina summed up the South's feelings on the matter. *"Without the firing of a gun, without drawing a sword, should they [Northerners] make war upon us [Southerners], we could bring the whole world to our feet. What would happen if no cotton was furnished for three years? ... England would topple headlong and carry the whole civilized world with her. No, you dare not make war on cotton! No power on earth dares make war upon it. Cotton is King."*

It is absolutely true that the South supplied the majority of the world's cotton. But the arrogance to think that the world would bow to the awesome will of the Confederacy if it no longer supplied cotton is outrageous! Not a single country bowed to the demands of the Confederacy, and the worldwide embargo of cotton only hurt the Confederacy. Obviously, those countries got their cotton elsewhere. To be clear, their first big idea the Confederacy had was to hinder the **only** thing that it had going for it.

I absolutely believe that Jefferson Davis wanted to return to the America that the Founders had envisioned, with a weak and powerless central government. The next great idea the Confederacy had was that, instead of demanding taxes to run the government, they asked politely. Almost no one gave a single cent. If anyone would like to see how a government runs without any taxes, look no further than the Confederacy.

Due to the fact that the Confederacy is a part of our shared history, it is even more important to make sure history is accurate! These guys were literally high off of their own farts. They believed the nonsensical tales of American exceptionalism. The Confederacy was a culmination of all the American fantasies.

This brings us to the next calamity that plagued the Confederacy: inflation. The Confederacy simply printed the money it needed. So when there was no money coming in from cotton or taxes, then they printed what they needed for everything...What could go wrong with that?

CONFEDERATE TREASURY NOTES[7]
Their Relative Purchasing Power in Gold

Date:	Notes Per $1.00 of Gold
1 May 1861	$1.05
1 October	$1.10
15 October	$1.12
15 November	$1.15
1 December	$1.20
1 February 1862	$1.25
15 February	$1.40
1 March	$1.50
15 March	$1.65
1 April	$1.75
15 April	$1.80
1 May	$1.90
15 May	$1.95
15 June	$2.00
1 August	$2.20
1 September	$2.50
1 February 1863	$3.00
15 February	$3.10
1 March	$3.25
15 March	$5.00
15 May	$6.00
1 June	$6.50
15 June	$7.50
1 July	$8.00
15 July	$10.00
15 August	$15.00
15 November	$15.50
15 December	$21.00
1 March 1864	$26.00
1 April	$19.00
1 May	$20.00

---

[7] Official Publication #13 - Richmond Civil War Centennial Committee

15 August	$21.00
15 September	$23.00
15 October	$25.00
15 November	$29.00
1 December	$32.00
15 December	$51.00
1 January 1865	$60.00
1 February	$50.00
1 April	$70.00
15 April	$80.00
20 April	$100.00
1 May	$1200.00

By the end of the Civil War, it would take 1.2K Confederate dollars to purchase a single dollar's worth of gold. The Southern economy was crippled from no taxes, inflation, and no cotton sales. It didn't matter how good the Southern Generals were, the economy was crushed by the end of the war, and the North wasn't to blame.

The next thing can only baffle you if you don't realize that the entire culture was awash in "American Exceptionalism." There were 5.5 million free people in the Confederacy. In contrast, the Union had 18.5 million. In order to overcome the disadvantage in numbers, over 75% of adult white males were enlisted to fight for the Confederacy. But there was an exception. One white man for every twenty slaves he owned didn't have to fight. Most of the white men in the South were yeomen. Meaning, they owned land but had no slaves. This created a class tension within the ranks of the Confederacy. The rich slave owners started the fight and they wanted the poor among them to fight it.

This same dynamic is still at play to this very day. It only makes sense if you believe that your whiteness is so special that you need to fight for it. They believed that one day, with enough hard work, they too could be like one of the rich plantation owners. I try to wrap my head around this and it still puzzles me. What were the yeomen fighting for?

The next shoe to drop for the Confederacy was the fact that they forgot about the women. The essence of this "can do spirit," is that a white man can do anything. Women were meant to stay in the home to cook and clean. There were about 2.75 million white women stuck at home starving. By the spring of 1863, the Confederate women took to the streets in a wave of armed food riots. These women raided government warehouses, army convoys, railroad depots, salt works, and granaries.

These women were the wives and daughters of the yeomen and were poor. To call this a miscalculation would be a bungle on my part. This was a serious blunder by the Confederacy! Women in armed revolt at home proved to be much more devastating than anything the Union did. The Confederacy then initiated a massive welfare program, rationing the limited food that they had between the soldiers and the wives. It's important to reiterate that the South made mostly cotton; they imported almost everything else, including food.

Which is another fantastic misstep. They produced cotton, almost exclusively. Then they cut off trade from Europe and the North. I'm confused about how they were surprised that they had food shortages. The selfish fantasy that they were better than the people that supplied their food is mind-boggling!

The last thing that the Confederacy struggled with was the position of the slave. It was a universal belief that the slave was unintelligent, subhuman, and the personal property of white men. You've got to understand, when I say that was an exercise in the fantasy of white supremacy, look no further than any word uttered by them about living, breathing people. They must've believed themselves gods among men. The problem with believing that the slaves were nothing more than cows came to a head during the Civil War.

Firstly, the Emancipation Proclamation was a giant threat for the South. There were 3.5 million slaves and they could revolt at any time and end the war immediately. The Confederacy needed to now divide its forces to combat against a potential slave revolt. But the problem of the slave came long before the Emancipation Proclamation.

Early in the war, slaves were found with guns and gunpowder, insurrection plots were discovered, and also chains of communication with the Union were found. This created a crisis of reality in the Confederacy. If the slaves were in fact people, then you would need to try these people for treason. Yet they weren't people, they were property. The property should be returned to its owner and he should deal with it. If the state does try and destroy the property, should the owner be compensated? If the Confederacy tries the slaves for treason, does that mean that they were citizens? It came as a complete surprise to the Confederacy that the slaves weren't on their side. This was a profound dilemma for the entire Confederacy. They were tried for treason.

As the war progressed, the Confederacy needed more troops and wanted to impress the slaves into fighting. The large slave owners protested, as they didn't want to donate their property to the war. It's fascinating that the Confederacy would even attempt such a thing. They asked the people who refused to pay taxes, and refused to fight in the war, to donate property. But the craziest thing about impressing slaves is the idea that they, the slaves, would in fact choose to fight for the Confederacy. If only the slave owners weren't so self-centered, we would have history on the lunacy of arming slaves and commanding them to fight for you. I can only say that these guys had to be totally full of themselves.

Close to the end of the war, two regiments of slaves were trained to fight for the Confederacy. It was approved by General Lee and the President. Even in the face of defeat, the Confederate Congress wouldn't allow any slaves to gain freedom for fighting for the Confederacy. Either they are human or they are not. They chose to lose the war with their personal beliefs intact.

Fighting aside, the Confederacy was doomed to fail. And it wouldn't have been decades or generations before their government collapsed, it would've happened in short order. When the Union won, the South was in shambles. Was this how the "Free Market" was supposed to work?

VELOCISSIMO – THE SPIRIT OF CAPITALISM

The Bid/Ask Spread and the Path to Zero

The markets seem to perplex the average person. The crux of what the markets are has existed long before the markets themselves were formally fashioned. The essence of every market around the world is the bid/ask spread. This is the price range for the exchange of goods or services for currency. There was a time when currency was intrinsically tied to a commodity of some sort. We won't consider the time when the currencies were tied to commodity, as it will only complicate matters.

The reason why it complicates things is that the commodities themselves also have a bid/ask spread. It is the hope of the people concerned that the underlying commodity's bid/ask spread doesn't fluctuate too much. If you wish to entertain the awesomeness of currency tied to gold, consider the Spanish Empire. The Spanish Empire was the dominant force in Europe until they traveled the globe plundering as much gold as they could carry. The rapid influx of gold collapsed their economy, giving an opening to the British Empire. Now English is spoken around the globe.

Q: What is the bid/ask spread?

A: The difference in price between the highest price that a buyer is willing and able to pay for an asset, product, or service, and the lowest price for which a seller is willing and able to sell an asset, product, or service.

There are some general misconceptions that I'd like to dispel now. First, you need to understand that buyers are desperately trying to drive prices down and sellers are doing their best to drive prices up. This is true for all goods and services, from the most expensive to the cheapest. Sellers of homes list their homes as high as they possibly can, and would go higher if they could. Just yesterday, in the middle of a heat wave, an elderly man asked the cashier at the deli I was in, "How much for this Icee?" "One twenty-five," the Arab man responded. The elderly man shook his head in disgust and tossed the Icee back into the freezer. Buyers want the lowest price and sellers want the highest price.

The next issue that people fail to grasp about the bid/ask spread is that spread itself isn't permanent. The bid/ask spread is directly dependent on two things. The first is supply and demand. If the supply of goods and services increases, then the buyers get to pick and choose where they'd like to spend their money. If buyers are in control, then the prices must drop. If the supply of goods or services drops, then buyers don't have a choice where to purchase. Sellers are then in control and they drive the prices up. If demand for goods or services increases, there will be too many buyers and not enough sellers. In this case, sellers are in control and prices go up. If demand drops, there are now fewer buyers. In this case, the few buyers that are there, have a choice in sellers; buyers are in control and prices drop.

The next issue of permanence that people fail to grasp is that all goods and services are affected by the flow of wealth passing through the nodes involved. To refresh your memory, the bid/ask spread is directly affected by the abilities, rates of change, and amount of currency in circulation passing through each person, business, or local government. Changing any of these things will directly affect the flow of wealth passing through each node. If the flow of wealth decreases through the nodes, then prices will fall. If the flow of wealth increases through the nodes, prices will rise.

Q: Isn't it better when prices are going up?

A: Prices going up or down aren't good or bad. They just are. Sometimes it is important that the prices go down, and sometimes prices need to go up. They aren't indicative of anything. People have unfortunately been conditioned to detest falling prices of anything. As usually it is followed by lost jobs and a financial collapse. They are also conditioned to love rising prices, as it usually means employment and the ability to buy things. A healthy balance is needed; neither is good or bad.

The last thing that people fail to understand about the bid/ask spread is that the good, service, or asset you purchased doesn't equal the currency you paid for it. Moreover, it doesn't equal the currency that others are paying for it. **Once you traded your currency for that thing, your money is gone!** I want it to sink in that whatever you own that you think has value is only an illusion. Your money is gone and the only time that thing has value is when you exchange it for currency again.

People believe that if they hold onto a thing long enough, someone in the future will trade that thing for more currency than the amount for which it was originally bought. While in general that is true, the reality is, the price of anything and everything could potentially go to zero. Whether or not you believe it to be true is irrelevant. Those comic books that you are saving, the house you are holding onto, the gold under your mattress, are all worthless until you exchange it. You believe they have value because there are people out there who are willing to buy these things right now. You can take comfort that there is currently a market for the things that you believe have value. But rest assured, the value of these things can go to zero. Even a cursory glance at history will illustrate this fact.

Axiom of the Markets – Fools Beware!

In this section there will be a lot of hurt feelings. I really do hope that I hurt you feelings if I'm describing you as a complete idiot. No, you don't have to reread that sentence. **I hope I hurt your stupid feelings!** But before I do, I need to clarify what an idea is. Ideas can be defined in many ways, but for our purposes, we'll define an idea as such:

Idea: An immortal thought, conception, opinion, fantasy, philosophy, etc., that leapfrogs through time and generations regardless of evidence to the contrary.

The ideas of the French Revolution persisted beyond the defeat of the French. With every subsequent financial collapse following the defeat of Napoleon, the people of Europe and America demanded expanded suffrage. Generations after the fall of Napoleon, people still equated royalty with failure. However, the truth behind the economic crashes can't all be attributed to poor decisions by the Royalty.

Another example of immortal ideas is that of the Confederacy. At the heart of the Confederacy was the belief that the South was financially supporting the lazy idiots in the North. The moochers in the North didn't understand the principles of the free market and didn't appreciate the hard working Southerners. There is a meme circulating on Twitter that, "1% of US citizens owned slaves in 1860."[8] What's fascinating about that statistic is that the same dynamic is still present. To this day, people embracing this view constantly spout the idea that they are financially supporting others, even though that view is demonstratively false. Moreover, these very people keep demanding "free trade" and less taxes even though neither will directly benefit them. Supposedly the South lost, but they really didn't.

The idea that seems to persist here in America, despite facts and evidence, is the idea that you should buy a thing that you think has value and hold it forever. I hope I offend you, because that is the single most stupid thing on the planet! No one, anywhere, who has any sense, would tell you to do that. Here is the axiom that I'm sure that you're heard before, but that hasn't seemed to sink in yet: **Buy Low and Sell High!!!**

I want to let you in on a little secret. The people who regularly buy low and sell high call those who buy and hold assets forever stupid. That's right, they call you stupid money. Those very same people do anything and everything to try and part stupid people from their money.

Now let's understand the motion of price. There are three phases that everything subject to the bid/ask spread is subject to: markup, consolidation, and markdown. I'm debating using images of stock charts here. I don't want to make this a lecture on how to trade. It will suffice for our purposes for you to understand what each phase is.

The markup phase happens when the supply or demand changes in a way that favors the sellers. The price gets marked up until either there is an oversupply or the demand is met. The consolidation phase happens when there is indecision or balance between supply and demand. The markdown happens when the supply or demand changes in a way that favors the buyers, and prices get marked down until demand returns or the supply has been met.

---

8   US Census 1860

Q: How does "smart money" utilize the three phases?

A: They have an entry and an exit strategy!

People who successfully navigate the various markets all have one thing in common. They know when they want to get in and when they want to get out. If you don't have a clearly defined entry and exit strategy for whatever investment vehicle you choose, then you aren't an investor, you are a collector. There is nothing wrong with collectors. But don't collect and talk about value! Don't talk about how you made a good investment, mention current prices, or talk about what you think is going to happen in the future. If you purchased a thing with hopes that it will go up in price, but have no entry and exit strategy, **you are an idiot**.

Q: What is selling short?

A: It is a necessary function in order to maintain liquidity in the markets. Selling an asset short simply means you can sell an asset at the current bid price and get money in exchange, all without owning any shares.

This may seem confusing at first, but it's still the same principle of buying low and selling high. In this case, you are selling high in hopes to buy low. The money you get in exchange for selling short is held by the brokerage. When you buy at a future date, if you sold short, you hope the price dropped. So you keep the difference from when you sold high and bought low.

In the fall of 2008, in the midst of a financial crisis, the US, Britain, France, Germany, Switzerland, Ireland, Canada, and many others instituted a temporary ban on short selling. I believe this was a result of the acceptance of the incredibly stupid idea that you should buy a thing and hold it forever. Moreover, they fail to understand who is actually causing prices to drop: the <u>Buyers</u>!

Stopping short selling will do the same thing every single time. It will cause the markets to cease. No one will buy or sell. Do you believe that the world would somehow be perfect if sellers kept selling higher and higher? There **always** comes a time when buyers are unwilling or unable to buy! Short sellers meet the demands of the buyers and supply them with what they want. Idiots holding on to a thing in hopes that the price turns around, and not short sellers, will stop the money from flowing and will destroy the markets anyhow.

The Smart Money

Some politicians continuously say that the stock market is unfair to regular people. The main reason is because the "smart" money doesn't buy and hold indefinitely. The "smart" money almost always profits. In fact, it got so bad that the government forced insiders of companies to declare publicly what they are doing.

Most Americans have their hard earned money in retirement accounts managed by large corporations. When you go to one of these places to put find out more, they give you a spiel about year over year returns. It's possible that those salespeople are a little invested in the thing they are trying to sell you. But guaranteed, none of the executives have a penny of their money in their year over year nonsense funds.

Would you go for steak at a restaurant where all the cooks are hardcore vegans? Then why do you think it's a good idea that your money is safe and secure in a company when none of the people running that company would put their money where yours is?

Let me explain the difference. The biggest players in the stock market aren't banks, corporations, or governments. The biggest players on the markets are the retirement accounts of Americans. The people's retirement accounts bring a steady flow of cash into the markets. In return, the people get a basket of stocks. Remember now…**your money is gone!** Each financial institution has their own proprietary algorithm to determine how and when to reallocate funds. These fund reallocations don't really follow price movements. In other words, they don't buy high or sell low. When you talk to a salesperson about this garbage, they get offended when you say anything about buying low or selling high.

The craziest thing in the world to me is that the majority of "wealth" in the markets is poor suckers leaving their money sitting there hoping and wishing that it will be there when they need it. Moreover, there is a strong push to put Social Security funds into the markets as well. How and why the entire country believes in a thing contrary to anyone who has any sense is mind-boggling to me. Jesus, it's the stupidest thing ever!

By contrast, the "smart" money doesn't do that. If you are mad at what I just said and you have a retirement account with a large corporation, then I'd like for you to do something. Go to your favorite search engine and type, "(Name of Company) insider transactions." (Name of Company) is your trustworthy financial institution. Given that it is public information, you have free access to it via the internet. The company that is supposedly making you money in the stock market has a history of insider transactions. If you are willing to spend a little money, you can go to a premium site that will chart the transactions for you. In any case, look over what the insiders are doing and compare that with what's happening with your retirement account.

These insiders are effectively betting against your accounts sometimes. This fact has come up in Congress a bunch of times. But they can't do anything, as the information is public. It's your fault for not noticing when the people managing your money are dumping their shares in their own company.

I have a feeling that I'm not doing this topic justice. Entire books are written just for this topic. It is really a shame that the nation's wealth is essentially held hostage in the stock market. First, it inflates stock prices. Secondly, the purpose of the stock market is lost in the staggering profits made. Please understand what I'm saying: **Your money is already gone**. The money of every American who put their money in the stock market is already gone. Americans are hoping that people will come forward and buy their stocks from them in the future. That would be a wonderful dream. It will happen, if and only if buyers are willing and able to purchase those stocks at a higher price.

Now politicians and pundits are trying to raise the retirement age. There will be a reckoning soon. What happens when enough people attempt to trade their stocks for money? Well, that will increase the supply of stocks in general. With increased supply, the buyers will be in control. Prices will plummet. Good luck, America.

The Function of the Stock Market

The stock market was designed for companies to raise capital in order to expand their business. There was a time in the past where banks weren't in the business of giving business loans. In fact, there was a time when banks were only allowed a 5:1 leverage on assets held. A business that would like to expand could go to the stock market, share their business plan with investors, and let investors know what the business will do with their money, if invested. A company then sells shares of itself on the open market and raises capital from those shares. With the money raised, they are free to initiate the plan they told investors that they would do. In time, if the plan bears fruit, the company can buy shares back or give investors dividend payments as a thank you. If they need more money, then they could simply sell more shares.

This is not how it works now. Companies that go public now, for the most part, don't need to raise capital. The want to "cash in" on the success that they've already achieved. There are two factors pushing the little guy out of the picture. First is the fact that small and large businesses can now get loans directly from banks or even from local governments. The second and biggest factor is all the "stupid money" in the markets. Pension funds buy and hold onto these stocks forever and ever.

I really hope that you are frustrated at me for railing so much against ordinary people having their retirement accounts in the stock market. There is a saying in poker, "Look around the poker table; if can't see the sucker, you're it!" In a letter to the shareholders of his company, Berkshire Hathaway Inc., in 1988, Warren Buffet said this, "Indeed, if you aren't certain that you understand and can value your business far better than Mr. Market, you don't belong in the game. As they say in poker, 'If you've been in the game 30 minutes and you don't know who the patsy is, you're the patsy.' " After much railing, maybe I should suggest a solution. I had plans to maybe do it myself, but I changed my mind. For now, let's see how the markets function currently.

Although companies can still simply sell shares on the open market, they usually turn to banks to make an initial public offering (IPO). Instead of competing, banks band together in order to mitigate risk. The banks and the company make an agreement of how much the shares would be bought and sold for. Once the deal is underwritten, the banks then go around the world pitching to large investors the prospect of owning shares in this IPO. They fill out the paperwork with the SEC and then pick an exchange to be listed on. The banks themselves buy the shares, then sell the shares on the open market, hopefully at a profit. Remember, the money that the banks are using is leveraged depositor money.

This is just the beginning of the joy for a potential company. Once the shares are on the open market, the company can then borrow money from banks using the shares it still has as collateral. Most companies opt not to sell more shares on the open market, because there is a possibility of a hostile takeover. Also, almost all executives take pay in the form of stock options. This is another way for the company and the executives to further avoid taxes, but is said to be an incentive to make sure executives focus on company profits.

To sum up, companies leverage themselves with already leveraged money from banks. You see how screwed up things are? The people put their money on deposit with banks and they put their retirement money in the stock market. Their retirement cash is traded for shares of companies and are held for many years. The companies in turn borrow money from banks, who are using leveraged money from the people. When things go south, the people get fired from their jobs and have little or nothing to show for it.

This unfortunate dynamic has set up a death spiral in our economic system. The stock market has become the heart-plug of the American economy. It is a place where the wealth of the nation can be instantly withdrawn. This unfortunate setup is why people hate when stocks go down, as they inevitably must do. If the value of a company's shares go down, then banks demand collateral for the depreciated share values. That is just the beginning of the contraction. Since most executives are heavily invested in the company, they usually opt to fire people in order to maintain profitability on paper. While it may make sense to them in that moment that layoffs are the right financial move, the problem is that the average citizen is the one that the entire system depends on. As people lose their jobs, less people will be sending money into the stock market, and spending less money in their local communities. Demand will wane, causing prices to fall, banks will demand money to compensate for the loss in stock value, and then businesses will fire people to cover the costs. A vicious cycle that has and will happen again. Nothing has changed.

A Potential Alternative for Average People

In 2008, I was scammed by a used car dealership. There were lies and forgeries. There was nothing I could do, as the company that scammed me was under investigation from the city. By the time I realized what happened, the used car dealership was shut down because of too many consumer complaints. I went to every venue possible, and was told time and again there was nothing that I could do. I spoke to a police detective after harassing the local precinct for weeks. He ultimately dismissed me and said, "Everyone gets scammed their first car."

I'm sure that I had a mental breakdown because of this. The only thing that soothed me was trying to figure out a way to get payback. After exhausting all of the violent options, I concluded that it was the financial system that enabled these scam artists. Then I put all of my mental energy into destroying the entire financial system. Impossible problems soothed me. Unfortunately, this problem wasn't as impossible as I wished it to be. I had already laid the foundation for the dismantling of the financial system with other problems that I had already worked out. So how to do it?

The first thing that you must realize is that the financial system that we have now has been obsolete for at least a generation. Unfortunately, the markets are intentionally confusing and people have accepted the hierarchy that already exists. Politicians fight the financial industry by regulating it, which only affects the industry temporarily. The finance people are fools, as they do as they wish believing the people have no other options. They lie, steal, and scam. It's like having a Cookie Monster in charge of the nation's cookies. How about we give the people an option and watch the too big to fail banks be too big to compete?

If I had about thirty-million dollars at my disposal, I would create a new bank. It would function under the same parameters as other banks do, except 70% of the profits, and most of the risk, would go to depositors. The bank would make its money from fees and 30% of the profits. I wouldn't aim to open up multiple branches. I also wouldn't sell lame products like certificates of deposit or savings accounts. So how would this work?

Let's say Timmy deposits $1,000 into my bank, let's call it the People's Bank. First, Timmy is given the 20:1 leverage that big banks say is unbearably low. Then Timmy is given a variety of investment opportunities to choose from, that the People's Bank has approved. To make it simple, Timmy wants to only invest in mortgages in his local town. The People's Bank will set maximum and minimum values to invest for every investment opportunity. For example, the minimum could be $20, and the maximum could be 1% of total account value.

Timmy decides to invest in 1,000 home loans at $20 each, thus investing $20,000 in bank money. If Timmy averages 4% interest with 30 year loans, every month the payment from borrowers will be $95. Of which Timmy receives $66.5 monthly, with an 80% annual return on investment for the next thirty years!

Q: How does the People's Bank make money?

A: The bank make profits from originating the loans and other products, and also from fees collected from depositors. People incorrectly assume that banking operations are free. They always cost money. But in return for free stuff from banks, the banks in turn leverage the hell out of your money. With the People's Bank, the only thing that will be free is air.

Q: Is it legal for banks to do such a thing? Aren't there privacy concerns?

A: If the question is, "Is it legal for banks to pay out money?" then the answer is a simple yes. Banks regularly give money out to their depositors. But it's almost always a joke compared to what they are making off of your deposits. The question of privacy is also a simple thing to solve too. All mortgage information is public. I can use an online tax record search or simply go to the County Clerk's office and request information about any house I want. The available information is the size of the loan, the bank who loaned the money, and when the loan was made.

With the People's Bank, I would make it company policy that depositors not contact any borrowers for any reason. If they do, they can be subject to financial losses. If the depositor defaults, we would proceed with it as would any bank, but most of the fees and losses would be absorbed by the depositors.

I would also have a secondary market, so that depositors can sell portions of their investments to others. If the borrower is current, I would allow borrowers to buy investment sales in the secondary market, which involves their specific loan.

Q: How can such a bank be financially successful? Wouldn't you make more money by just using borrower money to make money?

A: The People's Bank could potentially be more profitable than the way current banks operate. Why? Reciprocity, of course! It would be company policy to give individuals with proximity and connections first dibs at an investment. For example, a policeman in NYC would like to refinance his home in Brooklyn. He has great credit, a stable job, and never missed a payment on his previous mortgage. A few groups of people would get the first chance to loan money to this policeman. The first are the officers in his union. The next are his family members. The last are people in his neighborhood, with the people the closest to his home getting the highest priority.

So when this officer makes his mortgage payments, it will have a cascade affect in his local economy. The odds of that dollar returning to him shoot up dramatically, even though he's on a salary. At the very least, home values in his area will go up and there will be a slight increase in employment. Which creates more wealth. It's my belief that when people make more money, they will redeposit that money with the People's Bank. Quite possibly, the People's Bank itself would likely repeat the dollars passing through it multiple times.

Q: Will this Bank offer products in addition to mortgages?

A: This Bank will offer anything and everything other banks offer. Moreover, I would make it so that the "talent" that those banks have been grooming, will come to us. Banks offer liquidity to the stock market, capital for insurance companies, capital for proprietary trading, capital for IPOs, and on and on.

With the People's Bank, individuals, groups, and companies will be able to list what they have to offer on our site and the people will decide if they want to invest in it. Considering these investments are considerably riskier than mortgages, depositors will only be allowed to invest something like .1% of the account in each of these other types of investments. Also, no more than 10-20% of the account could go to these riskier types of investments.

The People's Bank would simply be an intermediary with financial interest. The People's Bank would qualify all of the investments and set rates. The people will be free to choose where to put their money. All types of insurance could be invested in, computer trading, proprietary trading, and so on.

If such an organization were to be created, ordinary people would leave the stock market and untrustworthy financial institutions in droves. There may even be an economic contraction. I think it would be a good thing to extricate the nation's wealth from the stock market. I think it's fair for me to offer an alternative if I'm going to insult you so harshly.

Such a bank would create firm connections between the smaller nodes, making the local economy far more stable. Doing things this way could potentially lead to a smaller footprint of government. But there will still be some pitfalls. Let's stay with the theme of misunderstanding the bid/ask spread and recall Tulip Mania.

The Bubble Blueprint

Talking heads love to claim that a bubble is coming. If we are to understand bubbles, then we need to look at the quintessential bubble: Tulip Mania. Bubbles of all sorts require two things. First, there needs to be product or asset that the public believes has immutable value. We know, or we should know, that this is never true. Secondly, you need ambitious speculators who believe in the immutable value of said product or asset. These speculators will fuel the entire bid/ask spread. Let's examine this.

While it's true that the axiom is buy low and sell high, this becomes warped with frenzied speculators. Speculators "know" that the price will go up so they buy the thing at almost any price. They buy with the plan of selling "when" the price goes up.

Q: If speculators are buying low and selling high, what is wrong with that? Aren't speculators what moves markets?

A: It is true that speculators move and maintain market liquidity. What I'm talking about is different. If there is an inherent belief that there will always be value in a thing <u>and</u> people blindly buy at any price "knowing" the prices will rise, then you have the blueprint of a bubble.

The issue at hand is this: Buyers are supposed to demand lower prices. If buyers clamor for higher prices, that is the beginning of potential doom. I say that it's the beginning because if they decided to all hold on to their purchases forever, then all is fine. The problem with speculators is that once they buy, they will be sellers within a short period of time. Things get worse if speculators are selling to speculators. Prices skyrocket until speculators are unable to buy. Although they may be willing to buy, the reality of purchasing power will make buying at a certain point impossible. That's when reality sets in and the only people willing to buy will pay pennies on the dollar for it.

Tulip Mania is highly illustrative, in that most people nowadays don't value tulips at all. Nonetheless, people in the past valued them, so it's instructive. Tulips were introduced to the Netherlands through trade with the Middle East. Tulips were found to be able to withstand the harsh climate of the Netherlands. In the early 1600s, growing tulips in your garden became a status symbol.

Tulip plants start as tulip bulbs, which do not flower for seven to twelve years. Between April and May, tulips bloom for about one week, with bulbs appearing between June and September. This confined Dutch sales to that season. Being a status symbol, people began buying future tulip bulbs, thus creating a futures market.

Once we have the futures tulip market and tons of demand from ordinary people, enter the speculators. Tulip bulb traders began to pop up all over. They would buy up all future bulb contracts and in turn sell them to other bulb traders at a higher price. This became a profession, as if tulip prices would simply always go up. In current US dollars, bulb traders made up to $61K per month.[9] While that seems like a lot of money, it isn't real money. The traders bought and sold from each other, causing the price to go up. In reality, they were playing musical chairs with the same little amount of money they started with. When the music stopped, only a few people had actual money, and the rest of the traders had a boat load of tulips.

The bubble popped when buyers were simply unable to buy any more. Once that happened, there was an army of people trying to sell tulips. The only people who wanted to buy tulips were those who wanted them for their gardens, and they were willing to buy the tulip

---

[9] "The Dutch Tulip Bubble of 1637," Allan Bellows, 2012.

futures at one-hundredth of their former price. In a matter of days, entire fortunes were swept away. To try and stem the financial crisis, the Dutch government offered to pay 10% of the future contract's face value, thus ending Tulip Mania.

This pattern has repeated itself a few times in the US. The problem that people don't understand is that stuff has no value until you exchange it. Your house, your stocks, your gold, and your tulips have no value. If you don't understand this, **then you are an idiot**!

FINANCIAL CRASH: A PRELUDE TO A FINANCIAL CRASH

The Victorious Confederacy

A couple of weeks ago, a young man entered a Charleston, South Carolina AME church and murdered nine people. The shooter hoped to start a race war. It's right now, July 3, 2015, and there is a push to get rid of the Confederate flags littered around the country. When people say that the Union won, do they even know what that means? The Union had one goal, to keep the States together, and it succeeded in this goal. Before the Civil War, people referred to their individual states as their country. Now, the country is the United States of America. Although the President still gives an annual State of the Union address, as if people need to be reminded that South Carolina won't attempt to secede again. The Union won, and now we are a united nation. I would like to remind you again that the Union forces were fighting to keep the states together.

What seems to stump everyone is why the South seceded. This is because the victors like to rewrite history and claim that they were so totally against slavery that they had to fight over it. Let's consider the reality of what the South was fighting for. Southerners were tired of supporting the lazy Northerners. The South clung to free trade principles and limited government, while the North wanted to protect its industries from being undercut by foreign products. If you hadn't noticed, it's the same arguments that we are having today.

Mitt Romney's candid 47% remarks were somehow a shock to people, but this is nothing more than Confederate beliefs leapfrogging through history. Southerners believed that they were better than the poor Northern states with high unemployment. Southerners believed that they made the world go around by being the biggest producers of cotton. Ninety-nine percent of Americans didn't own slaves. But most Southerners had their own cotton farms. They believed that the Northerners were mooching off of their hard work and at the same time belittling them for not understanding how the world works.

These feelings were codified in the Ayn Rand book, *Atlas Shrugged*. I admit to never reading this book or seeing the movie. I will likely never read or see them either. I have heard other people talk about it though. From what I understand about the book, all the hard working "producers" in America simply pack up and leave because they feel unappreciated. Or in other words…the Confederacy. Even the name of the novel, *Atlas Shrugged*, embodies the spirit of the Confederacy. Atlas was the Titan in Greek mythology whose task it was to hold up the world. The title suggests that people aren't appreciating the one who is holding the entire world on his shoulders, then suggests that Atlas put the world down — and watch how the world misses all his hard work. This is the embodiment of Cotton Diplomacy!

This ideology of American exceptionalism, or the belief that the United States is unique or exceptional when compared with the historical development of other countries, was never checked or challenged. Not even to this day. There is a push to remove Confederate symbols from government buildings, but there has never been a push to remove Confederate ideology. We all know what limited government and no taxes looks like, and it was called the Confederacy.

After the Civil War, we as a country adopted the strict laissez-faire approach to the economy. The Southern feelings of superiority continued as cotton was still king. Then through a series of legal maneuvers, slavery was over, the abolitionist movement was over, and yet the status quo remained. The Southern arguments won out in the end, as the North was mainly concerned with the Union. Extreme poverty and wealth disparities persisted.

Reconstruction – Southern Punishment

By the time Andrew Johnson had become the seventeenth President, it was time to try and heal the nation. The country was still divided, and Abraham Lincoln was assassinated. This period was called Reconstruction and it lasted from 1865 until 1877. Historians of the victors tell us that Congress passed the thirteenth through the fifteenth amendments to help freed slaves. They also tell us that they sent in the troops to ensure the rights and liberties of the slaves. But then they tell us that the troops gave up after ten years and left the former slaves to fend for themselves. I disagree.

Here is the reality. After the 1860 census, the states that fought for the Union had a comfortable majority in the house. The Union states had a majority of Senate seats as well, since some slave holding states remained in the Union. Even still, the votes in the House and the Senate for the thirteenth amendment were hard fought. Lincoln was reelected and in 1865 tried to end slavery. Let's consider the sides. The Democrats were furiously opposed to ending slavery, as they were all likely wealthy slave owners. The Republicans were actually still more concerned about the state of the Union.

Though Republicans were currently in the majority, why would they want to amend the Constitution? The three-fifths compromise benefitted them directly. Also, America was still in the grips of an economic depression due to cheap goods from India. Slave produced cotton was America's only financial bright spot. It seems totally righteous to believe that half the country was fighting for the suffering of the poor slaves, but I don't believe that to be the case. I believe politicians will be politicians in any historical time period.

The goal of the Republicans was to maintain the Union of the States. But consider who started the war and why. The war was started when wealthy slave owners decided that they were too good for the United States. The Civil War in the United States was started by approximately 1% of the population. Did these individuals lose anything? They didn't fight in the war, they didn't spend any of their money, and they didn't use any of their slaves. The rest of the South, on the other hand, was decimated. If I were a politician at that time, I would do exactly what they did then: strip those individuals of their financial power.

Accounting for inflation, the value of the all the slaves combined, in America, was over seven trillion dollars![10] The Civil War wasn't over; a ridiculous amount of wealth and power had to be stripped from the

---

[10] "Without Consent or Contract: Evidence and Methods" Robert William Fogel, Ralph A. Galantine, and Richard L. Manning 1992.

men who were still dividing the Union. The thirteenth amendment abolished slavery. The fourteenth amendment granted citizenship and equal protection under the law to freed slaves. The fifteenth amendment allowed the recently freed slaves the right to vote. All of these things were forced upon the South under threat from the US military.

Let's reiterate something that we all should understand. It was a given that people of color were sub human according to the majority of all white Americans. This didn't change after the Civil War. In fact, this is still something that is fought over today. None of the white men who ran the country believed that people of color were equal in any way to whites. Lincoln himself admitted as much. Then why would they vote to add these amendments to the Constitution? Why would Northerners throw away a guaranteed majority in the house by allowing the Negro to be counted as a person in the census?

This was all to <u>punish</u> the Southerners who fought the Union. Within those ten years of Reconstruction, freed slaves voted in droves and there were many recently freed elected officials. Most people of color were in the South, so it makes sense that this is where colored elected officials cropped up all over. I would say that the Northern states cared about the plight of the freed slaves if they were welcoming to them and asked that they come to their states. In fact, to this day, Northern states did everything possible to keep people of color out of their territories. When people of color did arrive in these states, they were forced to live separate from whites. Moreover, there was a dearth of colored representatives in the North.

The Emancipation Proclamation was a military tactic to defeat the Confederacy. I believe the thirteenth through the fifteenth amendments were political tactics to destroy and demoralize the Confederacy. I don't know how many times I have heard talking heads and pundits ask the rhetorical question, "Why did the US army leave the South just when the freed slaves had a modicum of dignity?" I hope that I've answered this question. Historians like to say that the government simply gave up trying to help the slaves. I believe two things were the real reason. First, there was a need to castrate the power of the people who started the war and to humiliate those who believed they were better than the rest of the country. Secondly, the US wanted the keep the freed slaves in the South so they could pick cotton. Ah yes, the cotton. At that time, cotton was still King.

Jim Crow the Superstar

What came after Union troops left the South was known as the "Jim Crow" laws. We will get to that in a moment. But it's very important to understand who Jim Crow was. In the early 1800s, a struggling actor in New York, named Thomas Dartmouth "Daddy" Rice, heard a black person singing this song:

> *"Come listen all you galls and boys,*
> *I'm going to sing a little song,*
> *My name is Jim Crow.*
> *Weel about and turn about and do jis so,*
> *Eb'ry time I weel about I jump Jim Crow."*

The history about who was singing the song itself is unclear. Some say it was an old black slave who had difficulty walking. Others say it was a poor stable boy. In either case, Rice had the brilliant idea of copying the song and creating a caricature of an African American man.

In 1828, Daddy Rice made his first appearance as "Jim Crow." Minstrel shows were popular back then as they were the only form of entertainment, in some areas. There were many minstrels traveling the country, but Daddy Rice will forever be known as the Father of Minstrelsy. Rice was one of the first to don the darkened face using a burnt cork. His Jim Crow character took him all around the nation and in 1832, he returned to New York with great acclaim. Rice didn't stop in New York. The popularity of Jim Crow was international. He even traveled to England and performed.

What you need to understand is that Rice had become an international superstar long before there were movies, recorded songs, or the internet. This was an incredible feat in the middle of the 1800s. He didn't stop with the Jim Crow character. He added new characters that were also exaggerated and highly stereotypical views of African Americans. There was Jim Dandy, Zip Coon, and Sambo. In time, people began to imitate these characters. Jim Crow, as well as the others, became stock characters in all minstrel shows. There were many traveling minstrels who entertained Americans in every state, with the beloved Jim Crow character.

Why is this important to recall? Because there are no recorded protests of Rice's shows. I have yet to come across a quote for almost a hundred years since Rice created his character saying that his caricatures

were false. Apart from a handful of abolitionists, white supremacy was the law of the land. More importantly, the vast majority of Americans were incredibly poor. Everyone worked long hours, from the young to the old. Here you see a photo of young coal miners working for a coal company in the early 1900s.

Nowhere, in any history books, is there mention of shared wealth or prosperity. The early history of this nation is defined by harsh poverty, extreme financial disparities, and rampant exploitation. For hundreds of years, America was supposed to provide the promise of a good life, if you work hard. America was supposed to provide the freedoms that other nations refuse to give. Yet, time and again the populace was faced with soul crushing poverty and slave labor conditions.

This is what made Jim Crow so popular and incredibly sinister. What it did was remind the white people in the nation that there were people worse off than them. Even though most of the country was illiterate, it felt good knowing that there were people less intelligent than they were. It was a great reminder, to the entire nation, of why the blacks were where they were and why the whites were where they were. Blacks were lazy, dumb, slow, and simple. More importantly, they were happy with their lot in life. The country needed Jim Crow. At least, the white people in the US needed Jim Crow.

The Jim Crow character and black-faced performances continued in the US for over a hundred years. While we don't have any recordings of Daddy Rice, we do have recordings of Jim Crow-type characters up until the 1950s. All the major recording studios used the Jim Crow characters in their movies and songs at some point. There's no point in wasting ink pointing any of them out. Feel free to peruse YouTube at your leisure if you'd like to find out more. I just want you to remember and realize that the white American psyche needed a constant reminder that they were special and important, despite the reality of their situation. Jim Crow was vital American propaganda. It is also important to note that these characters mostly disappeared from American culture in the 1960s.

The Birth of the KKK

If you are to believe the victors, the Union troops occupied the South in order to protect the rights of the freed slaves. We've already noticed that the wealthiest men in America had their wealth stripped from them. In fact, these individuals seem to be forgotten history. Over seven trillion dollars of wealth simply evaporated, and I can't for the life of me think of a single individual or family who any of that wealth belonged to.

In Tennessee, six Confederate veterans formed the KKK, as a joke. They thought the Greek word for circle sounded funny, kuklos, and whimsically formulated the name Ku Klux Klan. It started as non-violent stunts to frighten the recently freed slaves back in line. In time, others would join in the hijinks. They wore costumes to hide their identities from the Union forces and eventually the group became violent. The KKK spread through the former Confederacy, occupied by the Federal forces. There was no organized central authority. The KKK grew out of the white frustration at the freed slaves taking part in things that they weren't supposed to. As the popularity of the KKK grew, the Confederate General, Nathan Bedford Forrest, asked to join.

Forrest was a self-made man. He grew up in abject poverty with his 10 siblings in a two room cabin. He survived the typhoid that killed half of his siblings, including his twin brother. When he was 21, he left home to become a planter and a slave trader. He eventually became one of the wealthiest men in the South.

He was 40 when the Civil War broke out. He was made a General and had a natural gift for the art of war. He routinely defeated Union forces twice the size of his own. It wasn't just his military prowess, he had a gift for cunning and deceit. On multiple occasions, he tricked Union commanders into surrendering to his much smaller force, without firing a shot. He fought alongside his men, killing Union soldiers himself, and was also shot four times. His men respected and feared him.

What Forrest will always be remembered for was his attack on Fort Pillow. Forrest had at his command twice as many men than those at Fort Pillow. Also, half of the men fighting at Fort Pillow were escaped slaves. Nathan Forrest was known for his violent temper. When the soldiers in Fort Pillow refused to surrender, the angry Nathan Bedford Forrest left only a handful of survivors. The Union called it a massacre. This was the most controversial event in the entire Civil War. When the war was over, Forrest was taken to trial for war crimes. He was found not guilty, but was forever known as the Butcher of Fort Pillow.

When word got out the Nathan Bedford Forrest had joined the KKK, he quickly established himself as its leader. Before Forrest, the Klan was a disorganized group of disgruntled white men. After Forrest, the Klan became the "Avenging Ghost of the Confederacy." The Klan became a terrorist organization, but what were their goals? We can let Forrest answer that for himself: "I am not an enemy of the Negro. We want him here among us; he is the only laboring class we have."[11]

It is telling that the leader of a terrorist organization openly admits, in a newspaper, that he wishes to oppress the freed slaves. What was the federal response? This is where history meets reality. Once again, I believe that Federal troops occupied the South for two reasons, first to strip the people who started the war from power, and second to keep the slaves, no... freed citizens, in the South. Just when this terrorist organization began to form, the Federal troops packed up and left. Why? Cotton was King!

You may be skeptical at my assertion that the Federal Government allowed the KKK to exist and thrive, and that the Federal troops were there to keep the slaves from fleeing. But please remind me: In the almost one hundred years after the Reconstruction, which KKK member was put on trial for anything? What did the Federal Government do to crush the terrorist organization known as the KKK? The law of the land was that slavery was over. A lawless organization was necessary to keep the cotton flowing. It wasn't until the 1960s that the Federal Government lifted a finger. We will get to that later.

---

[11] "Interview with Nathan Bedford Forrest," Cincinnati Commercial August 28, 1868.

Jim Crow the New Way of Life

Once the Federal troops withdrew from the South, the white majority recreated the image of slavery through sheer brutality. The Southern and border states codified the Jim Crow laws. It wasn't just a series of laws, it was a way of life. A strict code of conduct that the people of color must adhere to or face brutal street justice. The use of the Jim Crow character, as a reference for the laws, demonstrates the type of people of color the South wanted. The fact that these laws existed from 1877 to the 1960s is telling about the wishes of the government, or the will of the electorate.

Jim Crow laws were established to clarify that whites were better than blacks. Blacks were banned from various job positions. Blacks were banned, through a variety of laws, from voting. Blacks were banned from certain buildings. The movements of people of color were strictly regulated. There were a plethora of laws, including social laws:

- Black men couldn't offer his hand to shake a white man's hand, as it implied social equality.
- Black men couldn't touch any part of a white women; if he did, it was considered rape.
- Blacks and whites were not allowed to eat together.
- Blacks were barred from public affection, as it was considered disgusting.
- Blacks were not allowed to address white people by their first names.
- Blacks had to always sit in the back of a car, truck, or bus if a white person was driving.
- White people always had the right of way while driving.
- Blacks can never assert that a white person is lying.
- Blacks can never suggest that whites are of an inferior class.
- Blacks can never claim to have, or demonstrate, superior knowledge or intelligence.
- Blacks can't laugh at a white person.
- Blacks can never comment on the appearance of a white woman.

There were a litany of these laws, most of which were enforced through the hooded Confederate avengers. If there was any confusion about where the Federal Government stood on any of these laws, the Supreme Court's famous Plessy versus Ferguson (1896) case legitimized the Jim Crow way of life.

The movements of blacks were severely restricted and so was job availability. As a "compromise," black people were "allowed" to sharecrop. Sharecropping was a system where the sharecropper rented land from a planter and paid the planter in crops. The South had its labor force back, and the cotton thus flowed again.

The people of color who didn't wish to accept a life in cotton were subject to brutal massacres and prison slavery. There were lynchings in the South almost every day. Most lynchings were a public spectacle to bring your family to. Lynchings mostly happened in small towns where whites were in competition for the same jobs as blacks. There were also mass lynchings in Wilmington, North Carolina (1898); Atlanta, Georgia (1906); Springfield, Illinois (1908); East St. Louis, Illinois (1917); Tulsa, Oklahoma (1921); and Detroit, Michigan (1943).

Even though this series of unfortunate events seems harsh, I believe that it was a blessing for the people of color. Why? Because the utter stupidity of laissez-faire economics and a single crop system was bound to catch up to the South one day or the other. While the people of color were still in bondage, they had some freedom to move from one place to the next.

Did Someone Order a Crash?

It may seem like I've gone off on a tangent, but the plight of the slave is highly relevant in our discussion about the flow of wealth. **The Panic of 1857** marked the beginning of our Civil War. **The Panic of 1866** marked the end of the war and the beginning of Reconstruction. Would it surprise you that what followed was another major international financial crash? **The Panic of 1873** happened in the midst of Reconstruction. Officially, the Panic of 1873 lasted between 1873 and 1879 and occurred in America and Europe. This panic was the beginning of a twenty year stagnation now called the "Long Depression." It used to be called the "Great Depression" until, well, you know.

The "reasons" for yet another global financial collapse are all the same. Sometimes they blame a single company. Sometimes they blame speculators. Of course, maybe large trade deficits, mounting war debts, or rampant inflation are to blame. It's rather annoying and patronizing to be fed the same lines again and again. There is a reason the deluge of economic crises aren't included in any American history books. People will stop accepting the same tired reasons for the crashes and begin to look at the system and consider that maybe it was the problem. Corporate interests will never want the nation's children ever thinking that there is anything wrong with letting the markets decide what's best for the nation.

Rather than focus on the "causes," let's observe the effects of the crash just for continuity. The economic crash set off a failure of multiple banks. Factories began to lay off workers. The New York Stock Exchange closed for ten days straight. Over 100 railroad companies failed or went bankrupt. Over 18K businesses failed, building construction was halted, wages were cut, and real estate values plummeted. Jesus! Now I'm being lazy. It's become so repetitive that I'm just rewording Wikipedia entries. But, isn't this what always happens?

We have a number of other crashes to get to, so I'd like to reiterate the problem. It is and will always be reciprocity. Wealth can't always flow in one direction. If it does, the wealth stops flowing and all of the above issues must take place. It always happens!

I wonder if the government planned to keep troops in the South longer than they did. You could say to yourself, "The US troops pulled out of the South due to budget constraints," but that is incredibly cynical. Why would the US government leave millions of its valued citizens in the hands of violent terrorists? It's easy: The government needed the cotton to start flowing again. The Panic of 1873 may have accelerated the end of Reconstruction.

The Panic of 1884 was somewhat averted when the New York Clearing House bailed out a number of banks at risk of failure. The "causes" bore me. Quite honestly, I would probably get upset typing propaganda. It's mind-boggling that there is always a rush to find the culprit that messed up the perfect system. If you want to look up the "causes," use the Google machine. But the effects should be known to us already. Over ten thousand firms and banks failed. This economic collapse wasn't so bad, huh?

The Panic of 1890, also known as the **Baring crisis**, also happened for some mysterious reason. This crisis spread throughout the world but didn't affect America too much. Well, there were bank failures and general recessions. Will you allow me to be lazy again? I'm just going to quote a quote from Wikipedia. *"The preceding year [in 1890], the great Baring failure had shaken London and the rest of the financial world. America was shielded from its most virulent effects because of a bountiful wheat crop. But the following year all the forces of business disturbance were assembling, though the country as a whole hardly realized it. Gold was leaving the country at an alarming rate."*[12]

The Panic of 1893, on the other hand, didn't really miss the US. Of course, history tells us that there was a reason for this recession. If only people would stop doing those stupid reasons, all would be right with the world! Alas, somebody did that thing again and there was a major recession in the US. I wonder what the effects were? (*Wink Wink*) According to the interwebs, stock prices plummeted, 500 banks closed, 15000 business failed, and many farms closed. There was widespread poverty and starvation. There are lots of other terrible things that happened but I don't know what excuse I can use not to write them. Do I want to not waste ink or are my fingers tired? Whatever.

Surprise! By the time the **Panic of 1896** occurred, the people became frustrated. Sure, of course there were "causes." Also, there were the usual effects of catastrophic deflation: declining prices for goods and services, dropping stock prices, bank failures, and job losses. The voters then elected William McKinley as the twenty-fifth President of the US. He was elected in 1896 and began his first term in March of 1897. He was an interesting choice as he was considered the Republican Party's expert on the Protective Tariff. It's a fascinating time in history. It's like the people themselves were attempting to reject laissez-faire capitalism. The only tool known to the people at the time was the Protective Tariff. Remember how the "Tariff of Abominations" almost caused the Civil War? What a difference a bunch of financial collapses make!

McKinley signed the **Dingley Act** of 1897 into law his first year in office. He was keeping his promise of protectionism. The **Dingley Act** itself raised tariffs that counteracted the **Wilson-Gourman Tariff Act** of 1894, which lowered rates. With protective tariffs in place, the stock market rebounded and the economy as a whole improved for a few years.

---

[12] John T. Flynn. "God's Gold: The Story of Rockefeller and His Times." (1932) p. 310

McKinley also decisively won the Spanish-American War. It would be the first true military win for the US. After losing, Spain handed over the colonies of Puerto Rico, Guam, and the Philippines. Also, under McKinley, the US annexed the Republic of Hawaii in 1898.

McKinley accomplished quite a bit while he was in office for those four years. It was a pivotal moment in history. The nation was exhausted from collapses and they trusted McKinley to lead them through. His policies didn't get much resistance from Congress. Unfortunately, there is a difference between the person running for president and the actual President. McKinley had accepted giant campaign contributions from John Rockefeller, JP Morgan, and Andrew Carnegie. People at that time were demanding campaign finance reform. For those people, I have to ask, when was the US presidency not strongly influenced by wealthy interests? Most of the electorate were recently granted suffrage; what would they know of fair elections?

The **Panic of 1901**, an interlude panic. Blah, blah, blah...some reasons. Stocks fell, people lost money and jobs. God, I didn't even want to mention this one. But it's interesting to note that protectionism didn't stop another crash.

There was at that time a Governor of New York named Theodore Roosevelt. He was spouting a lot of incredibly progressive ideas. Things like breaking up monopolies, conserving natural resources, and protecting consumers. He was the first politician who spoke of ideas to protect the working man from wealthy predators. What happened next is up for debate.

McKinley's vice president died while in office. Some say that Roosevelt's progressive voice made him the perfect choice to help McKinley run the country. Others believe it was a plot to relegate Roosevelt to obscurity, as the vice presidency, at that time, was considered a dead end position. Going from the Governor of a powerful state to Vice President was somewhat of a demotion. There is no way to really tell, but... upon reelection, McKinley decided to shift his policies of protectionism to the new and better idea of free trade. How did the Republican "expert" on protectionism start singing the praises of free trade? Could it have been the campaign contributions?? No one will ever know.

He was now advocating reducing tariffs and went on a nationwide tour proclaiming the wonders of free trade. On September 6, 1901, he went to Buffalo and gave a speech on free trade at the Temple of Music. While he was shaking hands after his speech, he was shot. He died a few days later. Who knows if the millions of dollars in campaign contributions had an effect on his policy decisions? Who knows if those very millions of dollars are what encouraged McKinley to take Roosevelt on as Vice President? What we do know is that Roosevelt was one of the best Presidents in our nation.

Roosevelt used his office as President to break up monopolies, called Trust Busting. His presidency involved attacking the plutocracy and helping the middle class, while at the same time protecting businesses from extreme demands from organized labor. Roosevelt championed food and drug safety and the conservation of the environment. He also started the construction of the Panama Canal.

Roosevelt really was a great president. He saw problems and aimed to fix them. To put things in perspective, the richest man in the history of the planet was a target of Roosevelt's: John Rockefeller. "By the time Rockefeller died in 1937, his assets equaled 1.5% of America's total economic output. To control an equivalent share today would require a net worth of about $340 billion dollars."[13] He wasn't the only one. There were a few other close behind him. The economic disparity at that time was grotesque and unimaginable. We are fast approaching those same levels.

Despite all his wonderful ideals and hard work, Roosevelt himself faced an economic crash in his second term. The **Panic of 1907** is also known as the **1907 Bankers' Panic** or the **Knickerbocker Crisis**. Again, I'm just not interested in the "causes," but I am interested in the effects known to us. There were significant losses in the stock market. Banks and businesses entered into bankruptcy. People lost their jobs and there were runs on banks. It's called the Knickerbocker Crisis because the Knickerbocker Trust failed. JP Morgan himself intervened and made the crash not as bad as it could have been.

Roosevelt was considered the first real progressive president in the nation. But it's fascinating that his progressive ideas didn't stop another incredibly intense financial crash. This is because the financial crashes happened as a result of the flow of wealth. Fighting for the middle class

---

[13]   "The Rockefellers: The Legacy Of History's Richest Man," *Forbes*, 2014.

seems altruistic, and will garner you votes, but doesn't affect the flow of wealth significantly.

The Wall Street Crash of 1929 and the Great Depression is where we stop for now. This was the worst economic collapse America has ever seen. This collapse spread all throughout the world and lasted about ten years. As usual, I don't care about the supposed "causes." For my purposes, the flow of wealth stopped. When wealth stops flowing, there is always cataclysmic deflation. With rampant deflation, prices drop, businesses fail, banks collapse, and unemployment skyrockets. The crash of 1929 was no different.

I'd do history a disservice by not looking at the forest from the trees. In my view, from the inception of the nation there was a deep financial crisis every few years. It is foolish to not address the elephant in the room and maybe suggest that the problem lies in our economic system. I say there was a problem. Just for shock value, here are all the financial crises since the American Revolution until the Great Depression:

- Panic of 1785
- Panic of 1792
- Panic of 1796-1797
- Panic of 1819
- Panic of 1825
- Panic of 1837
- Panic of 1847
- Panic of 1857
- Panic of 1866
- Panic of 1873
- Panic of 1884
- Panic of 1890
- Panic of 1893
- Panic of 1896
- Panic of 1901
- Panic of 1907
- Wall Street Crash of 1929 and Great Depression

If it seems like a lot, it's because it is a lot. It would be really annoying, and tedious, to relay to you the "causes" of all of these crashes. After a while, the "causes" don't seem believable. These crashes will never be included in any American History books, save the Great Depression, because they go against American Exceptionalism. I would applaud any history book telling the truth about American history. The truth is, between the years of 1776 and 1939, America can be characterized as in perpetual financial collapse, and its people existed in abject poverty. I doubt that any high school history book will ever teach that. How are we supposed to learn from history, if we are not told the true history? And finally, was Abraham Lincoln a prophet?

ADAGISSIMO – ANTI-CAPITALISM'S FAILURE

The Power of the Vote

The Crash of 1929 and the subsequent Great Depression bred a great deal of anger against the very rich, within the American populace. Yet the campaign for free trade capitalism still pressed on. Unfortunately, the populace had heard enough about capitalism. In fact, they put the blame of their economic woes at the feet of capitalism. Even with all the world, or more accurately, corporate interests, singing the praise of free trade and capitalism, the people had enough. There was a little war that we skipped, but first let's define capitalism.

> *Capitalism - an economic system characterized by private or corporate ownership of capital goods, by investments that are determined by private decision, and by prices, production, and the distribution of goods that are determined mainly by competition in a free market.*[14]

Capitalism itself sounds nice, but the application of it always leads to economic imbalances. We've talked about these imbalances at length. We've also looked at the history of free trade capitalism. It is mind-boggling that people still cling to this idea when it has never once been successful. Let's look at this little war.

World War I took place in between the Panic of 1907 and the Crash of 1929. I personally consider it a continuation of the economic crashes. Historians point to "causes" for the war as if those same things

---

[14]   Merriam-Webster Dictionary

reoccurred, we would have another global war. The fact is, the persistent economic crises were like the warnings of a global heart attack, yet no one listened. There was global poverty, and the world's wealth was held in only a few hands. Remember, the richest people in the history of the planet were alive during this time. It's amazing that the economic crashes are excluded from American history books. If they were not excluded, the cause of WWI would be made much clearer. When the money stops flowing, there must be an economic or a social collapse.

When WWI came to an end, the people were tired of free trade and were demanding protectionism. The Fordney-McCumber Tariff of 1922 was enacted by Congress and signed into law by President Warren G. Harding. The intended goal was to protect factories and farms from foreign goods. People attribute the "Roaring Twenties" to the enactment of this Tariff. While the tariff may have contributed a little to the prosperity of the time, I believe the country was in its last swell before a major crash.

Corporate interests weren't deterred by signs of prosperity or the wishes of the voters. In 1927, The League of Nations' World Economic Conference met at Geneva. The final report of this conference for the world leaders stated, "The time has come to put an end to tariffs, and to move in the opposite direction." No matter the time or season, people have for hundreds of years been preaching the idea that free trade is the cure for all things. Even though they tried to convince the world, and they had the ears of the most powerful leaders, most did the exact opposite of what this conference recommended. It was a real watershed moment for the world. It's like the world knew something was wrong, and the only thing it knew to combat the problem was protectionism.

After the Crash of 1929, the people were demanding higher tariffs. The Tariff Act of 1930, or the Smoot-Hawley Tariff, was enacted with great protest from the business community and thousands of economists. Even President Herbert Hoover was vocally opposed to the bill. Why did he sign it? Hoover was an incredibly unpopular president and had hopes of reelection. Shantytowns began to crop up all around the nation. They were filled with people who were unemployed and evicted from their homes. These towns were all called "Hoover Ville." To this day, economists believe this tariff went too far. In fact, the tariff itself was at the levels of the Tariff of 1828, or the Tariff of Abominations. The people weren't upset about it; only the elite were.

Alas, the tariff didn't help. What it did succeed in doing was that other countries then enacted their own tariffs. The voters still weren't pleased. The people had enough and were demanding change. Despite all efforts to the contrary, the people voted for Socialism in large numbers. In times of deep financial or social crisis, voters are willing to take a chance on something new. If the crisis is incredibly horrid, sometimes, the people allow tyrants to come to power. Without a fair vote, 1930 may have been a bloody time in the US. It is great fortune for us that we didn't elect a tyrant in our time of need.

Socialism Isn't the Antithesis of Capitalism

The appeal of socialism is on the rise in the US today. It has come to the point where a self-proclaimed socialist, Bernie Sanders, is a viable candidate in the upcoming presidential election. Socialism and communism have been maligned so much that most people aren't even clear what socialism or communism are.

> *Socialism - a way of organizing a society in which major industries are owned and controlled by the government rather than by individual people and companies.* [15]

Q: When did the idea of socialism start?

A: Some say around the time of the French Revolution. There are many references to social, or communal rule, for hundreds of years. The truth is that ruthless and unrestrained capitalism created socialism. Ordinary people were fed up with the greed and exploitation of capitalists, and literally created the opposite of capitalism. Or at least they think they did.

At first blush, you could say that with capitalism, things are run and owned by individuals for the sake of profit, and with socialism, things are run and owned by the government for the sake of the people. Clearly

---

[15]   Merriam-Webster Dictionary

they are polar opposites! Unfortunately, socialism cannot compete with capitalism. At best, socialism can slow capitalism down.

Q: How is socialism different from communism?

A: There is no real difference. Some say communism is a strict adherence to the tenets put forth by Karl Marx. In truth they are all different variations of the same thing. I'm sure there are communists and socialists out there who want it to be two different things. But, it's not.

Q: Why is socialism not the opposite of capitalism?

A: First, there never existed a capitalist government. Capitalism, in a pure form, can only exist briefly. The most capitalist government ever was the early US, and I would hardly call it a government. The US, before 1812, was nothing more than a collection of business interests. Businesses only care about profits, so there is no plausible way that those businesses could also govern.

While existing is the first challenge, the real challenge is in the application of both capitalism and socialism. The essence of capitalism is the bid/ask spread. Capitalists aim to buy goods or services as cheaply as possible, and then turn around and sell those goods and services at the highest price possible. Capitalists are constantly trying to find ways of production that will cut costs. The earliest incantation of this was slavery. Modern capitalists are vocally against slavery, and don't consider what the US did to Africans and their descendants "real" capitalism. Yet at the same time, these very same people utilize child and slave-like conditions all over the world. Capitalism demands the cheapest prices. Ultimately, this desire is its undoing. Total automation is the highest aspiration for capitalism. The moment androids are invented, the global supply chain will collapse and pure capitalism can never exist again. The "free market" only knows how to devour and consume.

In contrast, the application of socialism is somewhat diverse. First, of course, you have government ownership of some or all of the means of production. In this fantasy world, the government controls some or all of the jobs, and sets prices for some or all of goods and services. This can potentially be problematic compared to pure capitalism. The first problem is, What is the goal of the government? Are the institutions it maintains for the betterment of the people or for profit? Clearly, it's for the betterment of the people, right? The problem with this goal is the supply chain and the bid/ask spread. Neither the government nor the workers will have any motivation to make things better. Innovation will be stifled. In this respect, socialism will lose to capitalism every time.

The next apparent application of socialism is strict regulations. People who adhere to this particular philosophy love to point out successful regulations, or love to recall all the times when under strict regulations the economy didn't crash. These are all true, and of course regulations are important. But it appears to me that the go-to move for socialists is to slow things down to a snail's pace. Slower doesn't mean better. Slowing the markets down doesn't at all change the direction in which the wealth is flowing. Unfortunately, slowing capitalism down doesn't work. Eventually, the dam will break, either through legislation or innovation.

The next application of socialism is the vicious attacks on the rich. Socialism was born from the disdain of wealthy capitalists. Moreover, socialism in America came to power during a time of extreme anger at the wealthy. The antagonism towards the wealthy is and always has been palpable. This antagonism leads socialists to demand a "redistribution" of wealth. Some socialists, well, Democrats, try to preach redistribution without calling it redistribution. Some, like Bernie Sanders, are fine calling a spade a spade.

Q: Isn't redistributing the wealth good? The wealth will be flowing!

A: There are many problems with wealth redistribution, the first of which is a gross misunderstanding of what money is! Most money in our economy simply doesn't exist. There is no real point in taking nothing and giving nothing to someone else. If I could go to my bank account and see lots of zeroes, I would certainly be happy! That is an individual view. From the point of view of the government, it literally means nothing.

After the problem of most money not existing, the next problem is the flow of wealth. Redistributing the wealth will not cure structural inequalities. Once the money is spent, it will flow back to the same place it came from. This antagonistic nature towards successful people will hinder innovation and productivity. Now back to the application of socialism.

The last problem in the application of socialism is the imperfection of human beings. While capitalism itself is cold hearted and callous, it doesn't care which person is better than the next, as long as the wealth is flowing. At its heart, socialism is antagonistic towards at least some people. In America today, it generally is the rich. In other iterations of socialism around the world, socialism highlighted the divides amongst the people. This divide amongst the people would prove to be a real challenge for socialism in the 1930s in America.

The issue at hand is the flow of wealth. The government itself is nothing more than a giant node. If the biggest node in a local economy increases the flow of wealth passing through it, but changes the directionality of the flow such that some will never partake in that flow, then you will create massive relative deflation and potentially have an economic collapse on your hands. Socialism can only work with total unity among the people. This is an impossibility. People will always hate other people. These divides get exacerbated when capitalism entices part of the populace with the promise of great wealth.

I believe that there are many socialist ideals that we can incorporate into our society. I don't want to spend time here talking about this. It's very important that socialists recognize that there is no plausible way to compete with capitalism. There are a lot of well-intentioned people with big hearts out there that cling to the ideals of socialism as if it were an antithesis of capitalism. I totally agree with the things that you feel are right, but I wish that you all would realize that you are fighting a losing battle.

Let's consider an actual battle in NYC that just took place, in the summer of 2015. Bill de Blasio, the mayor of NYC, just picked a fight with Uber. There is a lot of noise over what is taking place. Given that right now I'm driving for Uber, I'm in a unique position to talk about it. The mayor is attempting to put a cap on the amount of cars a cab company can have in a base. In NYC, there are a lot of rules about having a taxi. One of them is that you need to belong to a base. I personally believe most of the rules surrounding taxis are simply a way to create income for the city. The base system is one of those things. Usually, a "base" is like a storefront, and people check in with the base for fares and such. Uber, itself, doesn't have any bases. But it has "affiliate" bases, or in other words, tax shelters. My Uber base is named "Weiter." I don't know where this base is, and have no clue how many other cars are registered with this base. While most cab companies have one base and a dozen or so cars, Uber has six or seven "bases" and thousands of cars in each of them.

Q: Why does Mayor de Blasio take issue with Uber? Don't they provide an excellent service?

A: De Blasio is facing what all socialists must face: the collapse of the supply chain! There are four concerned parties: the government, the consumer, the driver, and Uber. Drivers, for the most part, are happy. They are free to work as much as they want and can drive almost anywhere in NYC and pick up fares. As a result, many drivers are leaving yellow and green cab companies and switching to Uber. The riders love Uber because it's cheaper, reliable, comes quickly, and the cars are in much better condition than non-Uber cars. Uber loves the current setup in NYC; they pay little to no taxes, have almost no overhead, and none of the drivers are directly affiliated with them. The drivers pay for the cars, insurance, black car fund, and gas, and are in a quasi-contractor agreement.

The government is a different issue. There are hundreds of cab companies that are closing down in NYC. These cab companies operate out of storefronts and each directly employs a small number of people. When these companies go out of business, those people lose their jobs. To be clear, the city loses taxes and economic activity from the owners of the cab companies and their employees. Also, these actual bases pay rent and utilities. With the collapse of each cab company, a mini deflationary event happens and it is everyone's hope that new businesses will simply step in and fill the void left in the wake of dead cab companies. Companies like Uber lay bare the challenge of governing. The mayor of NYC has a peculiar problem to solve. He simply isn't equipped to challenge Uber in any meaningful way. The socialist answer of slowing it down really does nothing. De Blasio's attempt at limiting the rate at which a base can grow backfired, and he's backed off his proposal.

Capitalism will always attack the supply chain for a competitive advantage. Let's consider a future problem that NYC will face, and which Mayor de Blasio will have a similarly difficult time addressing. Let's say that the driverless car becomes available. In the beginning of this book, I spoke at length to all of the potential catastrophes facing our economy. But let's consider something that will hit home for me specifically.

I dread going to the barbershop. I always have to wait many hours for a $15 haircut. If you judge the barber experience from the movies, you'd think that there is some kind of camaraderie in a barbershop. Granted, there are inane conversations that I would never have anywhere else. But from my perspective, I don't know any of those people and wish not to talk with them! Then there is the dreaded empty seat barber. He's just waiting there, chatting everyone up, hoping and praying someone asks if he's free. Of course he's free! He's the empty seat barber!! Every single barbershop horror story of mine starts with me being impatient and taking a chance on an empty seat barber. So many painful lessons learned.

The day that driverless cars arrive is the day that good barbers won't be tethered to a local barber shop. I can easily imagine an app on my phone that will allow me to order a barber at a reasonable fee to come directly to my door and give me a haircut. I will get to pick and choose the best ones based on ratings and haircut examples. I also get to wait in my home until the barber arrives.

For the barber, he's making more money and doesn't have to pay weekly rental fees to any barber shops. He doesn't have to sweep any floors and he can literally set his own hours, and potentially travel the globe cutting hair. What about the local economy? Barbershops with small business loans will default. Thousands of barbershops will close down instantly, adding a large supply of retail properties. The losses in taxes and economic activity will be catastrophic for the city. What is the socialist response to this? Regulation?

Finally, let's consider something that I have no clue how capitalism will attack in the supply chain: mattresses. I like mattresses because everyone has one; well, almost everyone. Would you believe me if I told you that your thousand dollar mattress cost fifty to a hundred dollars to produce? How then does the price become so inflated?

First, you have the people who produce the materials to manufacture the mattress. The materials are transported and processed somewhere. They have a factory or a warehouse where these things get done. These factories employ a certain amount of people and pay rent and utilities. After the materials are ready, they are delivered to the factory where the mattresses are made. Most companies utilize shipping companies to deliver their goods. These shipping companies have a base of operations, which pays rent and utilities, and has a multitude of employees. Once delivered, the mattress is made and then sold in bulk to wholesale distributors. The finished mattresses are transported to the wholesale warehouse. The shipping company gets paid again. Also, the wholesale company pays rent and utilities, and has employees. Next you have local storefronts that display sample mattresses. These local storefronts have to pay a base salary and commission to their salesforce. Also, they pay rent and utilities. Finally, a mattress retailer spends money to advertise its available mattresses. The media company that took payment for advertising also pays rent and utilities, and has employees.

There are many points of ingress for a capitalist. With so many places to get a competitive advantage, it isn't hard to predict if prices for mattresses will plummet. It is quite easy to see the highest aspiration of a capitalist regarding the sale of mattresses. There will come a time when people will simply order their mattress online and the mattress is produced and delivered with minimal or zero human interaction. How does a socialist attempt to address this issue? Thousands of mattress stores, shipping companies, and wholesale companies will shut down across the nation. Raise taxes? Far too many people would have lost their jobs for a redistribution of wealth to be effective.

Q: What is the antithesis of capitalism?

A: Reciprocity is the only thing that can compete with capitalism.

The question shouldn't be about the size or scope of the government, but how many times a dollar spent repeats itself in a local economy. A diehard capitalist will say, "The market will correct itself, and new businesses will arise from fallen businesses." Unfortunately, this has never been the case historically. It is in the nature of capitalism to devour a local economy until all of the wealth is pooled into a few hands. The problem with capitalism isn't that it's callous or greed driven; the problem is that when a supply chain is collapsed, a capitalist blames those individuals for their own failure.

The goal of the government shouldn't be to pick and choose which industries to support, redistribute wealth to people who it believes are deserving, or to institute highly restrictive legislation. The goal of the government should be to make a dollar spent create between three and ten dollars of economic activity. In this way, it doesn't matter how capitalists attack a supply chain, a certain level of economic activity will always remain. Thus giving new industries a chance to bloom off the carcasses of dead ones. So that you understand what I'm trying to impart to you, in our example of the mattress, buying a mattress creates a lot of economic activity. The same dollar exchanges hands multiple times, through multiple businesses. If this supply chain collapsed today, the country could be in real trouble. Mark my words, the supply chain will eventually collapse and the only way to combat catastrophic deflation will be to have public policy supporting reciprocity, or an "artificial supply chain."

The Role of the Fed

A few years ago — I was 22, I believe — I had my first major mental breakdown. I dropped everything, quit my job teaching chess, locked myself in my room, and prayed and fasted. I prayed that I could be normal. I prayed that I could fit in somewhere. I got no answer. I decided that I would not stop praying until something changed. During the times that I wasn't praying, I searched the internet for people similar to me. I gravitated towards Christian conspiracy webpages.

Soon I was looking at websites that claimed to prove that the Federal Reserve had a secret agenda. One website would reference another website, and the next website would reference books. So I went to Amazon and ordered the books. I read the books, and they would reference other books. All the books and websites regurgitated the same conspiracy line: "The Fed is printing money and destroying the economy."

This information was frustrating for a man like me. I usually like some kind of proof. I noticed the "proof" always referenced somewhere else. So I went to http://www.federalreserve.gov/ to see what they had to say. I was even more confused. I found a phone number on the site somewhere and called it.

I was antagonistic to the woman who answered. I demanded she tell me how much money the Fed printed the previous year. She stated that the Fed doesn't really do that. This back and forth went on for a few minutes until I demanded she tell me what the Fed does if it doesn't print money. She let out a sigh of frustration and started talking. I would really love to relay to you what she told me, but… I had no idea what the hell she was saying. I appreciate that kind woman who spoke to me on the phone and I'm sure she wasn't customer service or a secretary. She tried her best to explain, but it didn't help. Plus, I was still acting like I was upset so as not to feel dumb. She finally suggested that she'd send me the data the Fed had on inflation for the previous year.

I waited a few weeks for this secret Federal Reserve information. I was so excited. I wondered if any of these conspiracy guys actually thought to just call the Fed? I didn't care. It was like the rainbow at the end of a stormy day. I couldn't wait!

Then about two weeks later I received a package. It was from the Federal Reverse addressed to meeee!! It was like Christmas in the summer. I ripped open the two packages. There were two phone book-sized books. In it were simply pages and pages of numbers on a spreadsheet. *What did this crap have to do with inflation?* I thought. I'm actually very grateful to all those conspiracy people. It gave me a very difficult problem to focus on.

I stopped reading the conspiracy books. I didn't know what books I should be reading. The internet searches that I could think of brought me back to the conspiracy pages with circular logic. I had to figure it all out on my own. That was exciting.

It's almost counterintuitive, but rest assured, civilizations have risen and fallen due to inflation and most people are entirely ignorant about it. Let's imagine a society with only ten people in it. There are also only ten thousand units of currency. It's the law; the society is strictly limited to ten thousand units of currency. Person #10 is the poorest and #1 is the richest. #10 has an idea for a show, but he needs ten currency units to make it happen. He approaches #1 and promises to give him 11 units after the show if he loans him 10 units. The deal is made. #10 gave a wonderful show. He charged two currency units for the show and everyone showed up. He made 18 currency units. He paid #1 eleven units and kept seven for himself.

Q: Was anything wrong with that?

A: No, the law wasn't broken. Simple lending like this doesn't add to the amount of currency in a society.

There are still only ten thousand units in this society and #4 and #5 gets married. They want to buy a house. There is only one house for sale, #3's home. The property is nice and costs 1K units. They both have good jobs working for #2. #3 gives them an offer; they can have the home if they make monthly payments to him. The terms are as follows: They have a 30-year note at 7% interest. The monthly interest and principal payments will be seven currency units.

Q: Was money created like this?

A: No. In 30 years, #4 and #5 would have paid a total of 2,395 currency units. But this extra currency happens within the context of the flow of wealth. No additional currency was created.

Q: How did banks come about?

A: The simple answer is safety.

Let's return to our Number society. Apparently, the Alphabet society is threatening to come and steal everyone's currency units. #1 creates a bank and tells everyone to keep their units there. He hires #9 for security and #8 as the banker. All ten thousand units are now safe and accounted for in the Number society bank. #1 promises everyone a 1% return annually for each deposited unit. In addition, each number gets a note of what the bank owes them.

Q: Has the law been broken?

A: Yes! The Number Bank promised to create one hundred currency units every year.

The Number Bank is growing. So is the Number population; they seem to really be multiplying. There are now thirty numbers. Decades have passed. The original ten thousand units have multiplied into one hundred thousand units. No one carries the currency units anymore; it's easier and safer to simply carry the notes. The Number Bank makes home loans, small business loans, and lines of credit for the purchase of large ticket items. All seems well, except #20-#30 don't really qualify for loans. They are left out of the lending and inflation is making them poor. The bottom third is simply in a credit desert. To make matters worse, there are rumors that the Number Bank and the Alphabet Bank are collaborating to maximize profits.

Q: What happens if all the numbers demand the units they are owed?

A: The Number Bank can only produce ten thousand currency units.

A rumor spreads that the Number and Alphabet Banks are secretly trying to steal everyone's money. All the numbers line up with their notes to get their currency units. The bank tells them that they need to get payment on the loans they had given out. In the end, the Bank is bankrupt.

There was a big debate about whether there should be a bank like the Federal Reserve; the arguments for and against it still rage on today. I'm not going to bother myself with those arguments for now. In addition, there are many theories to what caused the crash before the Great Depression. I read many of those arguments as well; not interested.

Q: Why were we removed from the gold standard?

A: Inflation would create gold that simply didn't exist. Gold can only work in a society where wealth doesn't change hands often.

The US Dollar used to equal 24.057 grams of silver. The US adopted a Fiat currency, not only in order to control the rate of inflation, but also in addition to make sure wages continued to grow with the inflation. If price increases outpace income increases, you'll have a collapse. If prices increase and income drops, you'll have a collapse. If prices increase and wages stay the same, you'll have a collapse. If prices drop and wages go up, business will lose money. Then businesses will fire people and cut wages and then you'll have a collapse.

Q: What does the Federal Reserve Do?

A: "The Congress established the statutory objectives for monetary policy — maximum employment, stable prices, and moderate long-term interest rates — in the Federal Reserve Act."[16]

The Fed has an incredibly difficult job. I for one am glad they exist. They are a regulatory agency whose job it is to oversee the entire economy. They track statistics from all around the country. The two phone books of info they sent me were the various price fluctuations in goods and services.

Many laws were enacted after the Great Depression. One was to make sure banks maintained a certain amount of leverage. Meaning, how much they can lend compared to what they actually have on deposit. There are currently people lobbying to remove these restrictions.

Q: Did inflation/deflation cause the Great Depression and Great Recession?

A: In my view, yes. Also, the lowering of taxes was a factor.

In the former, people didn't realize what happened. The government then created regulations and governing bodies to ensure the crash wouldn't happen again. In the latter, banks and investment firms lobbied and bought off regulators. Regulations eased, taxes were lowered, and leverage was increased.

I'm sure there are people who would be willing to debate with me on the "real" causes of these crashes — people with published books and fancy titles. They may even give me explanations that would take a while for me to understand. I'm sure that Credit Default swaps, subprime loans, and Ponzi schemes do have a part to play in the recent crash. In fact, I probably could write a three hundred page book just on those topics. It's been done before.

The first and obvious function of a bank is to protect the money of the depositors. They make it difficult for thieves to rob the money on deposit. Banks are then able to pool this money together and invest it somewhere else. There is an unspoken contract between banks and depositors that banks are good stewards of money.

---

[16]   http://www.federalreserve.gov/faqs/money_12848.htm

A bank has ways of evaluating potential borrowers. Banks have formulas that need to be met for each investment strategy. The largest banks pool depositors' money together and they gather talented individuals to invest this money. Home loans, business loans, and credit cards are some of the ways the pooled money is utilized. Some of the other ways are the Futures markets, Currency markets, Stock market, automated trading, and other things that I probably don't much understand. The profits made from returns from all these investments are then reinvested.

Somehow it appears profits are simply unlimited. What makes it even better is that some of these profits are used to lobby for less regulation. Bankers are called the "Masters of the Universe." For some reason they are uniquely qualified to move money that doesn't belong to them from one place to another. What fuels these investments is the FDIC guarantee that, up to $100K, the Federal Government will repay depositors in case the bank makes bad decisions and goes bankrupt.

In addition, banks regularly don't have cash on hand to give depositors if they ask for it. They are able to go to the Fed Discount Window and ask for short term loan. These loans are usually overnight, but the terms can be as flexible as 30 to 90 days. These short term loans are for a bank liquidity crisis. Without the Federal Reserve, banks would frequently not have enough money to give depositors if they need it. The Fed uses the rates in the Discount Window to affect interest rates of all the US banks. The Discount Window has helped keep the nation's banks from repeatedly collapsing. Unfortunately, not everyone has access to this magical Discount Window.

The Fed also has the power to increase or decrease its "balance sheet." In other words, the Fed can decide to increase or decrease the amount of available money at its discretion. In effect, the Fed can "print" or destroy money without actually printing or destroying any money.

Can an Economy Function if People are Paid to do Nothing?

I hope I got your attention with the title! It cuts right at the heart of the political divide. On November 1, 2013, four billion dollars were cut from the Supplemental Nutrition Assistance Program. The question is whether or not this is good for the economy. One side continuously demands that money from hard working Americans not go to people who don't deserve it. The other side essentially is making a moral argument. What I want to know is how this affects the flow of wealth and, can an economy survive payments being made without work being done?

As usual, both sides talk past each other. One side has heartwarming facts and the other side believes it knows what's best for the country. I don't want to keep you in too much suspense; I think the conservative arguments are technically and morally bankrupt. But I'm infinitely annoyed that liberals are constantly begging everyone to have a heart. Sometimes tough choices need to be made. Fortunately, SNAP isn't really a tough choice.

Q: Can an economy function if people are paid to do nothing?

A: Much to the chagrin of the people looking to demonize certain segments of the population, the answer is, quite simply, yes! Any society can set up a social agreement and pay some of its inhabitants, even if those inhabitants don't produce anything for the society. In terms of the flow of wealth, as long as each node spends most or all of the money given to it, in a given time, the flow of wealth is at least maintained. If a node spends all of the money quickly, the wealth is effectively multiplied. This is a point that I have attempted to explain multiple times. For now I'll just repeat a SNAP Fact.

Fact: Every $1 in SNAP benefits generates $1.73 in economic activity.[17]

At the heart of this fight is a sense of resentment. There is an idea that some people are undeserving of the help. There is an idea that wealth is going from people who work hard and deserve it, to the lazy and undeserving. This is also an issue of the flow of wealth.

Instead of assessing what has to happen now that the program was cut, let's talk about the rest of the groups not working and getting money in America. Of course there are retirees. Most people agree that they should be helped, but Republicans want to cut programs that benefit them as well. I believe non-production is at the heart of that

---

[17]   According to Moody's economist Mark Zandi

as well. There is a class of Americans who don't personally produce anything and make money: investors. There is even a subset of investors who are, in fact, economically destructive!

Our economy will survive with or without investors. Their very existence exemplifies the fact that an economy can function if people are paid to do nothing. Investors make their living shifting wealth from one place to another and paying people to do work for them. I'm not at all against investors, I just want to emphasize that people make money when not working, all the time. In fact, I suspect that most recipients of SNAP work more than investors. Yet for some reason, investors are praised and SNAP recipients are shunned. Work being done in a local economy is important, but the flow of wealth is far more important. Let's consider life before food assistance.

Everyone likes to point to the Great Depression to highlight their own views. While I am doing the same, I'd like to point out that catastrophic deflation similar to the Great Depression will always happen if the flow of wealth isn't maintained. Let's restate the three factors that stop the flow of wealth.

The reason why the wealth stopped flowing is at least one of these reasons:

1. The rate of change for specific nodes is greater than what is sustainable for the local economy.
2. Wealth is being diverted away from a local economy.
3. Nodes are forcibly removed from the local economy.

I appreciate the SNAP program because it serves as a backstop for catastrophic deflation. I have a challenge for Republicans who want to use the poor as a scapegoat. Given that if you cut the SNAP program you are dividing the wealth, explain how the subsequent deflation will help the nation as a whole? Most specifically, explain how cutting SNAP completely won't lead to Great Depression-style food lines? I'm annoyed that Republicans only deal exclusively in deflationary policies and Democrats in inflationary policies. Neither is better than the other! You have to apply both at various times.

Q: Is getting $1.73 in economic activity for every dollar spent a good ratio?

A: Liberals love to tout this fact as if it's amazing. When I hear such a statistic, I think the economy is anemic. Technically, if someone spends a dollar, that dollar could potentially change hands indefinitely. For example, I go and buy a candy bar for a dollar at a local store. I'm happy because I have a candy bar, and the store owner is happy because he just received a dollar from me. In a perfect world, part of that dollar will go towards taxes and part of that dollar will go towards goods and labor. The money sent to the government is supposed to go back into the economy and the money going to goods and labor will be spent in the economy as well. Effectively, a single dollar should flow indefinitely, producing an infinite amount of economic activity.

That unfortunately isn't the reality. The first issue is the rate at which wealth is exchanging hands. Some people spend right away and some hold onto wealth for years. Also, some people buy incredibly expensive things and some don't. Next is an imbalanced tax code. Some nodes pay little or no taxes. Not only does this subtract from the flow of wealth, it creates an imbalance in the flow that always leads to a crash. Finally, some money is simply diverted out of the local economy.

I would be impressed if a single dollar produced $5 of economic activity given a specific period of time. It would totally transform the economy.

How Would I Do It?

If I were President of the US and had legislative support, I would change the way we operate our economy. My focus wouldn't be on supporting specific constituents, or fighting for a particular lobbyist. The aim would be to have the dollar repeat three to ten times in every part of the nation. The first step is to create a system in which I can quickly track the flow of wealth from each node. All citizens, businesses, and state and local governments will be required to share their spending habits with an automated system. In the beginning, we likely wouldn't get any partner countries to join into the system, but it isn't necessary. We will be able to track the flow of wealth to and from various places in the world through the nodes available.

Q: Doesn't that violate laws of some sort?

A: Doing things this way likely violates a trade agreement or some antiquated laws promoting free trade. There will of course be naysayers who decry privacy. Also, let's not forget the Christian conspiracy people. This could well be the "mark of the beast." First, let me say this, people already voluntarily provide most or all of this information to the government every year during tax season. What I'm suggesting is that this information be organized and catalogued digitally. Also, the raw data can be accessed publicly. A citizen or a business can look at their spending habits and track the flow of their wealth. As for privacy, nodes can only access limited information on other nodes with that node's permission. All business and government nodes will be made public. This way, every node can make informed decisions about where to spend their money.

To be clear, a node's spending habits won't be made public. What will be made public is the economic relationship between nodes. For example, it would be nice to know the difference between buying a sandwich at Subway, Quizno's, or a local deli. What are the odds the money will return to me, how much would potentially return, how quickly it will return, and what was the local economic impact of buying each sandwich? This is all valuable information.

It's important to be able to regularly update changes in the flow of wealth. I would suggest that at least every quarter, new data should be publicly released, thus giving each node the chance to meet federal criterion. The Federal Government would set standards for how much each node needs to spend. For example, individuals and companies would be required to spend seventy percent of each dollar that they make locally.

Q: In what ways can the 70% spending requirements be met?

A: By spending money on any local product, service, or taxes. But there needs to be some clarification. First, spending money on the stock market wouldn't count. It produces no economic activity and can be used to unfairly divert wealth. Special considerations will be made for those who trade for a living. But simply put, the profits traders make on the stock market need to meet the same spending requirements.

Next are international goods and services. Every quarter, international goods and services will be given a multiplier based on their reciprocity to the US for that time period. Countries that spent more money on the US than we spent on them for that quarter will be given a high multiplier, and conversely, countries that spent less on the US than we spent on them will be given a low multiplier. For example, a candy bar from Canada and China both sell for $1 at a local store. But Canada may have a higher multiplier than China. If that is the case, a person will technically still be spending only one dollar, but each candy bar will affect the spending requirement differently. The Canadian candy bar may count as $2 in spending and the Chinese candy bar may count as ten cents in spending. Those who fall short of their spending requirements will owe significantly more in taxes.

Doing it this way gives wayward countries incentives to be actual trade partners. Pure protectionism can't work in a dynamic environment. If China wanted to change this scenario, the government itself could spend money in the US every quarter to make it economical for people to still want their products. Also, every node can invest in government bonds or in the People's Bank that I spoke of earlier. They can get solid returns at great leverage, but those returns will also be subject to the spending requirements. So if a company in China wishes to do business in America and China has a low multiplier, then the company itself can meet the given spending requirements. They can buy property, bonds, and so on.

The government will have a vested interest in improving the production of every node in the nation. With proper tracking, the government can accurately track areas of relative deflation. In these areas, the government can do two things. I would like the Federal Reserve to be able to increase and decrease interest rates locally, thus helping the Fed achieve its mandate. Next, the government will be able to increase or decrease local multipliers based on local deflation. Coming from the federal standpoint, changing local multipliers in the face of stupid State economic policy could be a challenge. I may need to skip affecting local governments economically. At least in the beginning.

Q: What about taxes?

A: First, I think taxes are too high and are incredibly unfair. The tax code is intentionally complicated so that very wealthy people can pay little or no taxes. Also, there are rules within the code that are targeted specifically at the rich. The giant and complex tax code is reflective of the partisan divide in the country.

Redistribution isn't a good goal for the tax code. Also, zero taxes is a Republican pipe dream. I would literally scrap every letter of the tax code. No one gets tax credits or handouts. Everyone would pay a flat rate, like 10%, for example. No 401k's, no oil subsidies, no child tax credit, none of that. The government would make up for the losses in taxes with reciprocity. If a dollar spent anywhere in America has an economic effect of three dollars, then a 10% tax rate is potentially 30%, but no one feels the considerable pain of paying that much.

Next is the Estate (death) tax. This tax came about due to public anger towards the uber rich. Just as soon as the law was written, a backdoor law was written so that wealth isn't seized and redistributed. In the last section, I pointed out that people not working is fine in a healthy economy. Wealth handed down from generation to generation is also fine. The only thing that matters is the flow of wealth. What I would do is charge individuals a small yearly tax proportional to their wealth, in lieu of a giant death tax.

First, the death tax has an arbitrary cutoff. It is clearly a tax unfairly aimed at those who are wealthy. I would have the cutoffs small and incremental. Also, I wouldn't start at death, but at retirement age. So, for example, a fifty-five year old who has $250K in personal assets. This person would potentially owe the government .1% of their wealth every year for the next thirty years. The increments could increase for every $10K in declared assets up to a maximum of, say, 1.5%. Meaning, a person with hundreds of millions of dollars would owe the government 1.5% of their assets every year. In this way, the wealth will continue to flow, and with proper investment strategies a person could potentially overcome this small annual fee. After thirty years have passed, the money remaining could be passed on tax free. If the person dies before the thirty years, his or her descendants will be given the choice to pay the remaining estate tax in full or continue paying yearly until the thirty years are up.

Doing things this way will erase all partisan bickering over the tax code. Also, the role of the government can and should change given varying climates. The size of the government is not as important as maintaining a healthy flow of wealth.

Reparations Nazi – Sorry, Mr. Coates, No Reparations for You!

"The highest economic growth decade was the 1960s. Income tax rates were 90 percent." - Bill Gates.

People from all walks of life look back to the 1960s as a turning point for the country. While different people look at this time and apply their own personal beliefs about why it was so awesome, the fact still remains that America had actually become a different country in the 1960s. I'm going to say something that I want you to engrain in your mind until the day you die. ***Before the 1960s, the US was essentially a third world country rife with economic depressions and extreme widespread poverty.*** For all my liberal friends, the New Deal didn't change the economic situation of the country much. But something happened in the '60s that changed everything, and sorry, Mr. Gates, it wasn't the tax rate.

Q: The labor movement changed the economic future of the country! You're wrong!! All the labor advances in the '60s were a continuation of the New Deal. If the labor movement is the cause of the '60s being so amazing, then the New Deal was the answer. What do you say to that, jerk?!

A: The New Deal, and the subsequent labor movement, were and are morally touching. Unfortunately, they aren't the reason for the American economic transformation. If you had been paying attention, you would already know what caused a sea change in America. But first let's look at the gains of the Labor Movement:

1. Weekends without work
2. All breaks at work, including lunch breaks
3. Paid vacation
4. Family & Medical Leave Act (FMLA)
5. Sick leave
6. Social Security
7. Minimum wage
8. 8-hour work day
9. Overtime pay

10. Child labor laws
11. Occupational Safety & Health Act (OSHA)
12. 40-hour work week
13. Workers' compensation (workers' comp)
14. Unemployment insurance
15. Pensions
16. Workplace safety standards and regulations
17. Employer health care insurance
18. Collective bargaining rights for employees
19. Wrongful termination laws
20. Age Discrimination in Employment Act of 1967 (ADEA)
21. Whistleblower protection laws
22. Employee Polygraph Protection Act (EPPA) — prohibits employers from using a lie detector test on an employee
23. Veteran's Employment and Training Services (VETS)
24. Compensation increases and evaluations (e.g., raises)
25. Sexual harassment laws
26. Americans With Disabilities Act (ADA)
27. Holiday pay
28. Employer dental, life, and vision insurance
29. Privacy rights
30. Pregnancy and parental leave
31. Military leave
32. The right to strike
33. Public education for children
34. Equal Pay Acts of 1963 & 2011 — requires employers to pay men and women equally for the same amount of work
35. Laws ending sweatshops in the United States[18]

It's hard to look at all of these things and say that they didn't significantly change the direction of the country. I admit that they helped, but it wasn't the deciding factor. This is a list of things that unions love to proclaim from the mountain tops as accomplishments. What I see are a list of regulations. I like these regulations, mind you, but these regulations do very little to affect the flow of wealth in the nation.

---

[18] Copied from UnionPlus.org

Q: What irrevocably changed the country in the 1960s?

A: The people of color were allowed to participate in the economy.

In fact, the biggest failing of the New Deal was that it excluded people of color. History books like to claim that black people were excluded from the New Deal because of protests from Southern Democrats. While that may be true, I don't seem to recall any defenders of blacks during this time. You see, the nation was still convinced of the supremacy of cotton, and the Negro was the cotton laborer. You want to know what really changed in the 1960s? The cotton picking machine became available worldwide!

Let's look at some facts. The first viable cotton picker became available in 1944 and was able to replace up to forty hand laborers. As with any technology, the cotton picker improved rapidly. By 1960, it literally made no sense to have any hand laborers picking cotton. Looking back, it was great fortune for the people of color that they were nominally free after the Civil War. It was also great fortune that the cotton industry began to collapse in the 1930s, forcing many people of color out of the cotton industry. It was also great fortune for the people of color that the cotton picker was invented. It depends on how you view it. These people suffered violence upon them, but I shudder to think what would've happened to these people had they still been the property of others when cotton no longer needed them.

It's funny how history books don't include the demise of the American domination of the cotton industry. It's particularly telling, the mood to which people of color engendered to the white populace as the cotton industry changed. After the Civil War, whites wanted to keep their laboring class. After slaves were no longer needed, their mood changed to, "Go back to Africa."

Q: What was the Great Migration?

A: History books tell us that is was the mass migration of blacks from the South to the North because of harsh treatment under Jim Crow laws. I disagree. First, both blacks and whites fled the South because of the death of the cotton industry. The fact that people of color were harassed, robbed, raped, and murdered wasn't new. Also, the Northern states were equally brutal to people of color. Both black and white people were involved with America's obsession with cotton.

Net Migration from the South, by Race, 1870-1970 (thousands)[19]

Decade	Native White	Black	Total
1870-1880	91	-68	23
1880-1890	-271	88	-183
1890-1900	-30	-185	-215
1900-1910	-69	-194	-218
1910-1920	-663	-555	-1,218
1920-1930	-704	-903	-1,607
1930-1940	-558	-480	-1,038
1940-1950	-866	-1,581	-2,447
1950-1960*	-1,003	-1,575	-2,578
1960-1970*	-508	-1,430	-1,938
Totals for 1940-1970	-2,377	-4,586	-6,963

I started this book detailing how the driverless car will destroy our country. I continued by stating that the steam engine played a major role in the Civil War. Now we see that the cotton picker nearly destroyed our nation in the 1960s. People, both white and black, were unemployed in mass. What is affectionately called the Great Migration should be called the Second Great Depression, or the beginnings of a second Civil War.

There was 18.9 million black people in 1960.[20] Given that most people of color were share croppers, I wonder if the unemployment data of the time reflects the masses of people ejected from the cotton industry. According to government data, the unemployment rate was only 5.5% in 1960. I honestly find that hard to believe. Activists nowadays bemoan the fact that people aren't as "fired up" as they were during this era. Not being able to feed your family has a way of firing people up.

---

[19]   United States Bureau of the Census, Historical Statistics of the United States: Colonial Times to 1970 (Washington: Government Printing Office, 1975), Series C 55-62, pp. 93-95.

[20]   U.S. Census Bureau

Q: How did the collapse of the cotton industry change the US from a third world country into an economic powerhouse?

A: It wasn't the cotton picker itself that did this. In fact, the cotton picker quite nearly ripped the nation apart. What changed is the collective opinion of the US on how to handle the Negro problem.

People look back at the Civil Rights Movement as the time when the country finally dealt with its problems of race relations. While it's nice to believe that racism was solved back then, that wasn't the issue at hand. The nation, as a whole, had an elaborate system to maintain the racial status quo. When the cotton industry didn't demand hand laborers any more, those systems of control had a real problem. The nation had a labor force of close to twenty-million and nowhere to put them.

Blacks were excluded from working or living in places all around the country. But by excluding them, these people were forced to take action. It is also great fortune that a leader arose and taught non-violent opposition to those laws of exclusion. There are scores of Americans that owe their lives to Martin Luther King. Quite frankly, he stopped a bloody revolution. His path of non-violence entailed public shaming of racist policies. This strategy is still employed today, but with far less effect.

The cotton picker didn't do anything but lay bare the foolishness of white male supremacy. The people in power had a real dilemma. How do you deal with the blacks? There were really only two choices: genocide or concessions. Given that the Labor Movement had tied itself to the Civil Rights Movement, genocide was not really an option. The powers that be had no choice but to grant people of color equal rights.

Q: You didn't answer the question! How was the US economically transformed?

A: I just said it. Equal rights changed the economic fortune of the nation. From an economic perspective, zeroing out the nodes of millions of people is an extreme deflationary factor on the country.

The fact is, white male supremacy has been the primary cause of the economic suffering of the country since its inception. The universal effort to keep the people of color as unpaid laborers did nothing but make white people poor. White supremacy itself became a self-fulfilling prophecy. Whenever black people entered a local economy, it was a deflationary event. Thus proving the inferiority of the race. The improvement of the lives of the people of color was the main cause of America's economic fortune.

Some of you don't believe me. Some of you are thinking I'm trying to pull a fast one on you because I'm a black man. You look around your nice neighborhood and your good job and say to yourself "I did this." There are still people all around the nation who actively want to keep people of color away from their jobs and neighborhoods. Your fancy job and nice house are a direct result of the change in the economic fortunes of the nation's giant slave class.

Such a thing is nearly impossible to prove without data, as no one save me is saying that the economic fortune of the nation shifted as blacks gained wealth. But to prove it to you without data, let's do a thought exercise. I want you to consider your job, housing, and any opportunities afforded to you. Now imagine all blacks voluntarily decided to revert their status in society to a time when they were either slaves or slave-like. To even things out, people like Oprah and Michael Jordan giving up their wealth will cancel out the debts of poor blacks. We do this so that no one is owed money when the blacks revert. They all voluntarily file into "work camps" and work for little to no money. They all do this voluntarily and happily, so there's no need to feel guilty. I have a question for you. Would this change your economic fortunes at all?

The first issue is jobs. The loss of the economic activity of blacks will create a giant deflationary event. In 2015, the buying power of African Americans reached an all-time high: 1.1 trillion dollars.[21] The fact is, part of the income from your job is directly proportional to the economic activity of people of color. Many people will be downsized and everyone else will likely take pay cuts. You think your house is awesome? Before the 1960s, no one wanted to buy homes because of the constant crashes and no real economic value to them. Blacks had no role in the housing market? What do you think will happen when the blacks vacate the large cities? What do you think will happen when that one black

---

neighbor you have leaves? Those vacancies will cause a deflationary event all across the nation. It was originally terrifying to see brown people move into your neighborhoods, but it turns out they were a financial boon.

Purposefully excluding millions of people from the economy obviously hurts those people. But more importantly, it hurts everyone else as well. Blacks being integrated into the economy had a significant multiplicative effect on the economy.

Q: Should black people get reparations?

A: That's almost a trick question. If the question is, should special accommodations be made for people who this country has systematically wronged? Then the answer is yes. I think those accommodations should address how to increase the flow of wealth to those people. But if the question is, should a payment be made to people this country has wronged by financially benefitting from their labor? Then I would disagree. Why? **Because neither this country, nor the vast majority of its citizens, ever benefitted financially from the subjugation of blacks**.

This seems like a salacious statement given that anyone can pull up records of the nation and many people making a living off the backs of slaves. In fact, the US received tax dollars when American cotton was sold. This is not what I'm trying to impart. I'm saying that slavery made the entire nation poor. Slavery cost the government money. Slavery was never a financial boon, but more like an economic vise.

Even after all this time, you still don't believe me? Let's try a different mental exercise. The slaves were about ten percent of the population back then. Let's imagine there exists today a population of androids, numbering ten percent of our population. Imagine, if you will, the state of our nation if there existed over thirty-million robots, capable of replacing human labor. What does our nation look like? Would you even still have a job? How about your friends and family, are they unemployed? How many of your neighbors will file for bankruptcy? Do you think your home value will remain stable? If our modern economy couldn't withstand a giant robot slave labor force, what makes you think the nation fared any better a hundred years ago?

As for the reparations, the thought of it disgusts me. Of course I'd love a government check right now. Getting the money doesn't disturb me; what disturbs me is the constant desire to have what whites have. In the '60s, it kind of made sense that the people of color asked for what they were intentionally excluded from. Yes, there is still some level of exclusion going on in our society, but demanding what whites have does nothing but reaffirm the inferiority of blacks.

For example, in NYC we have a housing program where poor people can sign up to get incredibly cheap housing in luxury high rises. People are selected by a lottery for this program. I find this program repulsive. It reaffirms this meme that if only the poor can be around the wealthy, things will magically work out. This theme is in our media, laws, and general thinking. The problem isn't that blacks don't have access to what whites have; the problem is that people who look like me are generally excluded from the flow of wealth. Unfortunately, people don't realize that this is the thing that makes everyone poor.

Recently, Ta-Nehisi Coates wrote a piece in *The Atlantic,* making the case for reparations for people of color. I have to admit that I didn't read the entire thing. Not because I wasn't interested, but every sentence filled me with such sadness that I couldn't bear it. Part of me wonders how he waded through the muck of what is American history. But I am doing the same thing now, and I feel equally troubled. It bothers me even more that no one is talking about this stuff as if it isn't really our history. His long piece didn't even focus on the brutality of slavery, he focused on the time after 1960.

Mr. Coates brilliantly made the case that white people made incredible financial gains from that time until now, and people of color were purposefully excluded. I can't argue with his logic. But I do take issue with the premise. White people didn't gain wealth at the expense of blacks; on the contrary, whites gained wealth because black lives improved. This notion, that black lives would be better if only they got some of what whites have, has been going on for hundreds of years. People of color have been fighting and struggling forward and need to look back at the gains we've made. Of course things could be better, but wanting what whites have does nothing but reaffirm white supremacy.

Reparations wouldn't be the answer. If a check was handed to black people across this nation, the wealth would flow out of the black communities as the wealth flows now. What really matters is the flow of wealth. If a tangible flow of wealth begins to pass through communities of color, the nation's collective fortunes will change.

THE RISE OF SOCIALISM

The First 100 Days

Most people don't realize how severe the Great Depression was. When historians say unemployment was at thirty percent, the reality of local deflation doesn't really register. Consider this: By 1933, Toledo, Ohio's unemployment was eighty percent and Lowell, Massachusetts was close to ninety percent. Before the New Deal, the people never expected the government to help in a crisis. After the New Deal, it wasn't whether the government would help, but how it would help. Even though it was Congress that enacted the laws, it was Franklin Delano Roosevelt who pushed them. The role of the president made a significant shift during FDR's tenure. Even today, no one looks to the legislature for laws; they ask the president what he would do. The nation depended on FDR, and he was the only president elected four times. After he died in office, Congress enacted the twenty-second amendment to the Constitution, limiting the presidency to only two terms.

The New Deal shifted the political landscape. The Democrats had a permanent majority, with a liberal base, white Southerners, and labor unions. The Republicans toed the line of limited government and saying the New Deal was hurting business and growth. This Democratic coalition dominated the government from the '30s into the 1960s. The New Deal was incredibly controversial back then, but the collapse of the economy needed something different. Here are the things that were enacted in the first 100 days:

- March 9 - Emergency Banking Act
- March 20 - Government Economy Act
- March 22 - Beer-Wine Revenue Act
- March 31 - Creation of Civilian Conservation Corps
- April 19 - Abandonment of Gold Standard
- May 12 - Federal Emergency Relief Act

- May 12 - Agricultural Adjustment Act
- May 12 - Emergency Farm Mortgage Act
- May 18 - Tennessee Valley Authority Act
- May 27 - Securities Act
- June 5 - Abrogation of Gold Payment Clause
- June 13 - Home Owners Loan Act
- June 16 - Glass-Steagall Banking Act
- June 16 - National Industrial Recovery Act
- June 16 - Emergency Railroad Transportation Act
- June 16 - Farm Credit Act

Emergency Banking Act

"I can assure you that it is safer to keep your money in a reopened bank than under the mattress."[22]

The first problem the new administration needed to address was that no one trusted banks any more. It was the banks that had foreclosed on their homes and businesses. It was the banks that had somehow mismanaged their money. People were afraid that if they put their money in a bank, it could magically disappear. They were right to be afraid. Any catastrophic deflationary event, at that time, must necessarily involve banks, as they are a primary way wealth is inflated.

The Emergency Banking Act aimed to stabilize failing banks and instill public confidence in the banks themselves. The day after FDR was inaugurated, he declared a four day bank holiday. All banks, including the Federal Reserve, were closed.

FDR sent the Emergency Banking Act to the House and demanded that they pass it right away. It was done in such a rush that there was only one copy of the legislation and most people voted on it without reading it. When it was rushed over to the Senate, they read the legislation out loud so people knew what they were voting on. While I can understand the urgency, the rushed nature of this legislation goes against how a bill is supposed to be passed. There was no debate or input.

This act expanded presidential authority during a financial crisis. It also granted further power to the Comptroller of the Currency, Secretary of the Treasury, and the Federal Reserve. People don't recall that Congress had given much of its power away to the Executive

---

[22] President Franklin Roosevelt in his first Fireside Chat, March 12, 1933

Branch. What they do recall is that the government guaranteed 100% of all deposits in all US banks. After this act was passed, there were lines of people waiting to deposit their money into a local bank. Also, the stock market posted the single largest gain in its history. This could be considered a success, but guaranteeing deposits simply allowed banks to take on more risk.

Government Economy Act

FDR was desperate to balance the federal budget, so he got Congress to pass the Government Economy Act. This Act cut the salaries of government employees and benefits to veterans. The liberals in the legislature apposed this act. But FDR turned to conservative Democrats and Republicans to pass this law. Even back then, balancing the budget meant cutting services to Vets. But his commitment to doing anything and everything impresses me. Cutting the pay of all government employees was bold. There is no way to cut your way out of an economic tailspin. But, "A" for effort.

Beer-Wine Revenue Act

The prohibition of alcohol proved to be difficult to enforce, given the state of law enforcement at the time. The only thing that the prohibition of alcohol did was create well-funded, organized criminal enterprises. The Beer-Wine Revenue Act legalized beer and wine and taxed the sale of beer and wine to raise revenue. A few months later, the twenty-first amendment officially ended all prohibition on alcohol. The prohibition of alcohol is similar to the prohibition of drugs. Even with our modern law enforcement, there is nothing that we can do to stop people from using drugs.

Civilian Conservation Corps (CCC)

The CCC was the first time that the government itself put people to work for the sole purpose of revitalizing the economy. Most of the CCC work was in the unpopulated West and only employed young men between the ages of 17 and 23. Most of these young men left their homes and lived and worked at CCC camps. These young men planted almost three billion trees, fought fires, built and upgraded hundreds of parks, took part in pest eradication projects, constructed roads, built lookout towers, and strung telephone and electric wires. The CCC provided shelter, clothing, and food. The workers were paid $30 per month, $25 of which was sent to their families. The money was meant to stimulate the local economies hardest hit by the depression. This program was ended when WWII started, as those very young men were called to fight in Europe.

This program was considered to be a success, but it unfortunately adversely affected people of color. First, there was a limit placed on how many blacks could join. The limit was 10% because that was the percentage of the population of blacks. Unfortunately, people of color were hit the hardest during the Great Depression. Scores of blacks were being ejected from their sharecropping jobs. In addition, the few jobs available were deemed "whites only."

Even though the program started with a non-discrimination clause, when people began protesting interracial camps, all of the camps became segregated. To make matters worse, the CCC allowed local officials to choose who would be selected for the CCC, and blacks were often passed over. There were over three million young men enrolled in the CCC, 250,000 were black. Honestly, even though it wasn't really ten percent, it was better than nothing.

Abandonment of Gold Standard

Britain had left the gold standard in 1931 and FDR followed suit. The problem was that people all around the country were hoarding gold, thus keeping the wealth from flowing. If everyone today decided to stop spending money, our economy would collapse just as it did in the '30s. The gold standard can't be sustained in a fast moving economy.

Federal Emergency Relief Act

The Federal Emergency Relief Administration started with $500,000,000 to help the needy and unemployed. After two years, three billion dollars were distributed. The three goals of the FERA were to be effective, provide work for employable people on the relief rolls, and to have a diverse variety of relief programs. The Relief Administration was taken over by the Social Security Board in 1935.

These funds were provided from the Federal Government and allowed local administrators to distribute the funds. Scores of people were put to work, but the African American was largely left out.

Agricultural Adjustment Act

The AAA paid farmers not to plant seeds or to kill off excess livestock. The intended purpose was to stabilize prices as catastrophic deflation caused prices of all goods and services to plummet. This was the beginning of farm subsidies in America. I personally think this was a silly idea, but times were desperate and FDR simply wanted to pay people for anything and get the economy moving. It is important to note that, again, most people of color who applied to the AAA were denied assistance. In addition, by paying farmers to produce less, blacks were simply expelled from the land as sharecroppers were not needed.

Emergency Farm Mortgage Act

The Emergency Farm Mortgage Act was passed alongside of the Farm Credit Act. US farms were almost all going into foreclosure. Things got so bad that the farmers formed their own militia and began to shoot at law enforcement. This militia was called the Farmer's Holiday Association. This group did things like block roads to keep produce from getting to the markets, thus starving the nation until the foreclosure crisis was addressed.

Under these two acts, the government essentially forced local banks to refinance the loans on local farms. Saving local farmers from immediate liquidation was just the beginning. The Farm Mortgage Act encouraged farmers to not plant on sections of their land; again, in hopes of increasing the price of produce. The EFMA also purchased produce from those very same farmers and distributed it to schools and the poor. Most blacks didn't own farms, so this program didn't affect them.

Tennessee Valley Authority Act

This was created to oversee the construction of dams to control flooding, improve navigation, and create cheap electric power in the Tennessee Valley basin. To this day, the TVA is the largest power company in the US.

The TVA had to flood 730,000 acres of land to make a new dam. Over fifteen thousand people were displaced. All the farmers received cash settlements for their condemned properties. Sharecroppers received nothing and were forcibly removed from the lands. Most of the tenant farmers were black.

Securities Act

This act was the first federal legislation aimed at the regulation of securities. The Securities Act aimed to ensure transparency in financial transactions, and to establish laws against misrepresentation and fraudulent activities in the securities markets. This act compelled financial institutions to disclose pertinent information about securities, so that investors could make better informed decisions.

Abrogation of Gold Payment Clause

This made it so that paper money became legal for the payment of all debts, public and private. In fact, this is printed on all currency now. This clause abrogated — annulled — gold payment clauses in all contracts. Abandoning the gold standard was simply not enough, given that people had contracts that demanded gold. This aimed at correcting this.

Home Owners Loan Act

This act formed the Home Owners Loan Corporation. The HOLC was tasked to refinance the mortgages of homeowners facing default due to the Great Depression. Farm properties, homes worth more than $20,000, and properties with more than four units were excluded. The HOLC would buy the troubled loan from a local bank with government bonds financed by the Treasury, then give the troubled homeowner a new loan. The HOLC had lent out about $350 billion dollars, and owned one in five mortgages in America by 1934.

During the Great Depression, there were about one thousand foreclosures per day. It made sense that the government stepped in the try and stop this. Unfortunately, the HOLC frequently denied people of color assistance.

Glass-Steagall Banking Act

This act was named after two congressmen during the Great Depression. People tried to understand why the economy crashed, and concluded it happened because of "improper banking activity." This would be spot on if you consider the Great Depression a one-time event in our history. The reality is quite different. There were many cataclysmic economic events in our past. The Great Depression simply was the most severe.

Let's consider what Glass and Steagall called improper. Commercial banks would buy stocks in a company, make loans to that very same company, and then turn around and encourage the depositors to buy shares in that company. The money used to buy shares and issue loans was leveraged depositor money. This of course should be illegal, but to say that it caused the economic collapse is a stretch.

The GSA (Glass-Steagall Banking Act) created a barrier between investment banking activities and commercial banking activities. Banks were given a choice to do one or the other, and only 10% of a commercial bank's total income could come from securities. The aim of the GSA was to prevent banks from using deposits to cover investment losses.

Liberals point to the GSA as a regulation that really works. In 1999, Congress repealed the GSA. Liberals like to blame the repeal of the GSA for the collapse in 2007. I would like to disagree. What the GSA does is slow the rate of change for the flow of wealth. Repealing the GSA did nothing more than increase the rate that money changed hands. It's important to be able to control the rate of change for wealth in an economy, but having a strict regulation that does nothing but restrict is damaging. The government should have a way to increase and decrease the rates of change in the economy, and this can only happen if the government has a way to track those rates.

National Industrial Recovery Act

The National Industrial Recovery Act was FDR's most aggressive tactic. He wanted to pursue the principles of socialism in the US, and this is the closest that he got. His reasoning for doing this act was sound: He wanted to raise prices for goods and services after the severe deflation of the Great Depression. This was supposed to stimulate the economy. The NRA (National Recovery Administration) and the PWA (Public Works Administration) implemented FDR's National Industrial Recovery Act. These agencies were tasked with

regulating <u>every</u> industry in the US. They set the price for goods and services, and they dictated the amount of money workers were to be paid. They guaranteed the rights of unions, and many unions were formed during this time. These agencies told businesses what business they could engage in and what business to avoid.

Most people are unaware of this period in our history, but we are aware of its aftermath. Republicans to this day fight unions as if their lives depended on it. It would've been interesting to see how long such a system could last. Unfortunately, the NIRA was declared unconstitutional by the Supreme Court. This eventually led to a standoff between the President and the Court. A Constitutional crisis, if you will. While that may be exciting to relay to you, it's a simple matter for you to search "FDR court packing" and delight yourself with our storied past. I'm concerned about the flow of wealth and like to wonder about the effects of the NIRA.

First, let's consider the people at the bottom. The NIRA hurt people of color. Are you surprised? By this time in our history, the yeomen of old were long gone. Most of those white Southerners lost their land in one of the many economic collapses since the Civil War. When people think of sharecroppers, they usually imagine a poor black family. The reality was that about two-thirds of all sharecroppers were white and the rest were black. These white sharecroppers were called "Rednecks," as they spent their time in the sun farming and were usually tanned. The social status of Rednecks was the same as the blacks, even though there still existed laws that stated blacks were still less than whites.

The NIRA allowed the sharecroppers to unionize. The unions in the South were looked at as an abomination. First, because whites and blacks organized together for a common goal, and secondly, it challenged the "natural order." There were many intentionally unfair rules in place for sharecroppers. That they weren't allowed to sell the things they grew without the land owner's permission was one of the biggest issues. Sharecropping was a legal way of keeping the sharecroppers in severe debt and essentially working for free.

The terror campaign that ensued for those who challenged the system was brutal. Whites that challenged the system were taken to court and blacks who challenged it were murdered by mob violence. Even in the face of violence, sharecroppers did strike. There was a problem with unionizing sharecroppers: Cotton was no longer king. The utter stupidity of our past is mind-boggling. Our obsession with cotton knew no bounds. As America expanded west, so did cotton farming. This cause a severe overproduction of cotton, which might have had a greater effect on the Great Depression than economists admit to. In addition to this, due to America's constant bragging about how awesome cotton was, other countries began to grow cotton. The US didn't have a monopoly on slave labor. Who would have thought that by writing books, public policy, and songs about how awesome cotton was, others would think to copy us? *"I wish I was in the land of cotton, Old times there are not forgotten; Look away! Look away! Look away! Dixie Land."*[23]

The unionization of sharecropping failed miserably. The result of the strike led landowners to evict scores of people of color. I think it was ultimately a good thing for them, but in the short term it made blacks even poorer.

Another unfortunate side effect of the NIRA was that it created a black market. I wonder how long this would have lasted had the courts not struck it down. I wonder how FDR would account for the goods and services sold that people hid from the government.

Emergency Railroad Transportation Act

This Act created a Federal Coordinator of Transportation to administer collaboration by the railroads in order to end wasteful spending and return the railroads to profitability. The law put aside antitrust laws and allowed cooperation among railroads and gave the coordinator authority to enforce participation by all railroads. The railroad companies fought efforts to end overhead costs by consolidating routes or services, and the law had little impact on returning the lines to profitability before it ended in 1936.

Farm Credit Act

This Act created the Farm Credit Administration, 12 Production Credit Associations, 12 Banks for Cooperatives, 12 Federal Land Banks, and a Central Bank for Cooperatives. These things still exist. The farming industry was in disarray and needed emergency cash.

---

[23]   "Dixie" by Daniel Decatur Emmett

Socialism Spreads to Germany

Anti-Capitalism Engulfs the World

It's difficult to take the mainstream media seriously when you check facts for yourself. Take, for instance, the oft-repeated phrase, "We are now an interconnected global economy." Those words, or combinations of them, are repeated on the news every time the stock market dips in any part of the world. Can you call it willful ignorance or a flat out lie? The reality is that the global economy has been interconnected for hundreds of years. While America suffered through the Great Depression, the rest of the world also suffered.

It was a global deflationary crisis. For some reason, money no longer existed. No one could afford to buy anything. This may not be the history that people like to recount about our planet, but it was as if the entire world said with a loud voice, "No More Capitalism!" Socialism spread throughout the world in various forms. Different groups chose to brand their particular socialism in different ways, but it was all the same thing in varying degrees.

In Britain, it was called "The Great Unrest" and lasted between 1910 through 1914. During that time there were mass strikes, riots, and rebellions. In response to those uprisings, Britain sent in their armed forces. That did nothing but fuel the unrest. The greatest benefit of a democracy is the people's ability to express themselves through voting. This led to the rise of the Labor Party and the adoption of socialist ideals in Britain.

The Chinese Communist Party was founded around this same period in 1921. Their rise to power is just as interesting as any party's rise. The CCP's dominance over all of China came from fighting a war against Japan and ultimately a civil war. The CCP called it the War of Liberation, and that rise to power took over twenty years. Similarly, in Russia, in 1917 there was a communist revolution. Why? There was widespread poverty and chronic food shortages. It almost seems unfair to sum up entire histories in a few sentences. But I want to impress upon you that the world was in a state of flux, and it was a direct result of global catastrophic deflation. The global conflicts themselves were a direct result of the financial imbalances created by unchecked capitalism.

Germany was no different from any of the other Western powers. What took place in Germany was special and requires the attention of the entire planet. This book started with a premise that I thought up over a decade ago, and I knew very little of history before researching for this book specifically. There seems to be a global consensus that Hitler was an evil man, the worst ever. Honestly, ask yourself, what do you know about Hitler? It is beyond fascinating that the history of this person was never explained to me. Hitler was a talented human being caught up in the events of the time. The catastrophic deflation that created an opening for FDR also opened the way for Hitler. But before we look at Hitler's rise to power, there is some public confusion over whether Germany suffered from inflation or deflation.

The Worst Recorded Inflation in History

The hyper-inflation that plagued Germany had in fact subsided by the time Hitler officially came to power. The period of hyper-inflation had stabilized just before the global depression hit. The combination of them both was an intense stressor for the German people. Let's consider how the inflation itself happened.

Germany's financial woes started during WWI. They made a gamble, betting it all on a quick victory. They chose to use the printing press to finance the entire war. They reasoned that this gambit would pay dividends once they won the war. During this time, Germany had a problem similar to that which the American Confederacy had. The people were itching for a fight, but the central government didn't have much power to tax the entire nation.

In order to hide what the Reichsbank, Germany's central bank at the time, was doing, a massive propaganda campaign ensued. The German stock exchange was closed for the entire war, so that no one would suspect anything was wrong. The currency exchange rates were also not published. Germany tried slogans to get people to donate to the war effort, to no avail. In the same way the Confederacy was defeated, so was Germany. Would history have changed dramatically had Germany not decided to finance their war with the printing press? A major contributing factor to Germany losing WWI was the fact that men were withdrawing from the battlefield in droves to go home and support their families. The rise in prices for goods and services crippled the German economy.

After Germany lost the war, the Treaty of Versailles was imposed upon them. As a condition of peace, the Allied Powers, mainly

France, declared that Germany was responsible for the entire war and was required to pay impossible war reparations to the Allied Forces. In addition to this, part of Germany was annexed and Germany was ordered to reduce their army size by seventy-five percent. As a consequence, a quarter of a million Germans were forced into an already soft job market. The Weimar Republic had little choice but to continue printing more money.

By 1920, prices had inflated twelve times higher than they were before the war. The Reichsbank may have believed that they had gotten the knack of that inflation thing. While the rest of Europe was struggling to get by, Germany had an incredibly low unemployment rate, and people seemed to be generally happy. Inflation and deflation aren't good or bad, they just are. The Reichsbank thought that it could manage the economy with pure inflation.

Germany's Central Bank simply increased its balance sheet, meaning they lent out lots of money. Businessmen would borrow money from the Reichsbank, at low interest, and buy almost anything. They would buy things like stocks with money borrowed from the Central Bank, and the stock market soared. Companies were happy with their stock prices and gave their workers more money. It didn't take long for people to realize that prices for goods and services were going up faster than they were getting raises. So the people began buying up products the moment they received their paychecks. Germany was the envy of the world, stock prices soared, and products were moving off the shelves quickly.

Before I go on, I'd like to point out the parallels between the Reichsbank and the current Federal Reserve. After the election of Barack Obama, the Republicans vowed to oppose anything he proposed. Given that there was no legislative way to address the financial crisis we were in, the Federal Reserve took it upon itself to help the economy. It too expanded its balance sheet, effectively printing money, just as the Reichsbank did. The Fed called the trillion dollar expansion "quantitative easing." What was the difference then and now? The first difference is that the Fed is aggressively tracking prices across the country. They used their own data to ensure inflation didn't rise too rapidly. Secondly, and most importantly, most of the money the Fed issued never reached ordinary people who would spend the money.

As we discussed earlier, the rate money exchanges hands has a direct result on how much money exists in a local economy, and consequently, on the inflation rate. In the last ten years, the wealth of the top one percent of the nation increased by almost seventy-five percent, while everyone else either stagnated, dropped, or raised slightly. This is because the people at the top simply don't spend money. They don't have to. America isn't plagued by the inflation of Germany because the rich don't spend their money, and if they do, it's with other rich people. Hence the term, stagflation.

In Germany, on the other hand, money was exchanging hands so rapidly that there were shortages of money. In order to keep up, the printing presses needed to go into overdrive. Things were moving so quickly that workers needed to be paid three times per week. Wages continued to increase and so did prices for goods and services. Because Germany was making reparations with worthless paper, France lost patience and demanded that part of Germany be occupied to make up for the payments. The Allied Forces then took control over the Rhine ports of Duisburg.

While the rich in America didn't spend the printed money they received, the rich of early twentieth century Germany had incentives to spend. The German government imposed high taxes in order to help its ailing budget. The rich simply opted to defer paying their taxes and spent their money in any way possible. The rich during this time were literally drunk with excess. Their reasoning for deferring taxes was sound. Given the pace in which inflation rose, by deferring tax payments, they effectively reduced their tax burden. By paying at a future date, the government would be given marks that were essentially worthless. This hurt the poor and the middle class the most as they couldn't afford to defer tax payments.

The rush to buy reached a fevered pitch in short order. Stores were sold out of goods, and farmers refused to bring goods to the markets. The economy had collapsed due to hyper-inflation. There were mass bankruptcies, assassinations, riots, protests, and strikes. It was so bad that the workers who printed the money went on strike. Out of frustration, France then occupied the Ruhr region in order to get goods and services in lieu of paper money. There was then a country-wide strike in protest of the French occupation.

There were food shortages, layoffs, bankruptcies, and the like. What ended the inflation is just as surprising as it is instructive. The entire inflationary period was between the years of 1914 and 1923. The value of an actual gold mark went from a one to one ratio to the paper mark in 1914 to a billion to one ratio in 1923. In November of that year, a new bank was created, the Rentenbank, and they issued a new currency, the Rentenmark. The public was told that this new currency was backed by land and properties. To everyone's amazement, the inflation subsided. Even the mark itself stabilized.

You may be wondering how that happened. If you were paying attention, then you'd already know how. The hyperinflation happened because people were spending the money quickly, thus adding to the amount of money. The Rentenmark was not backed by anything. It was a ploy to try and stabilize the economy. I want to impress upon you again that the money we have only exists because we agree that it does. I don't know when the term "consumer confidence" was first used, but it's clear that German hyper-inflation was a direct result of people not agreeing to believe in the currency.

One final thing happened to the German people before Hitler rose to power: The government declared Germany a military state and suspended its constitution. Germany became a military dictatorship, with a socialist cabinet, and was divided into seven military districts. The State of Emergency was called because of the mass strike against France. The army forced people back to work.

Hitler: The Little Soldier that Could

September, 1919, Corporal Adolph Hitler was ordered to go under cover and investigate a group known as the German Worker's Party. As you know, during this time there were many uprisings. Marxists were known to want bloody revolutions, and the German army was actively involved in crushing Marxist uprisings. The name of the group made it suspicious to the army.

The German Worker's Party met in the back of a bar and had about twenty-five people. The group was there for a talk on economics by Gottfried Feder, called, "How and by what means is capitalism to be eliminated?" After the talk, Hitler began to leave when a man spoke up and declared that Bavaria should break away from Germany and combine with Austria.

Upon hearing this, Hitler was fuming. He angrily proclaimed the incorrectness of that man's statements and spoke uninterrupted for fifteen minutes straight. Hitler's passionate speech impressed one of the group's founders, Anton Drexler. He gave Hitler his book entitled *My Political Awakenings*, and asked him to return to the meetings.

Hitler read Drexler's book the next day in his barracks and found that Drexler held the same views as he did. They both believed in a strong nationalist, pro-military, anti-Semitic party made up of working class people. A few days later, Hitler received a letter asking him to join the executive committee of the party. Initially he was reticent about joining the group. In his book, *Mein Kampf*, Hitler describes the group this way: "Aside from a few directives, there was nothing, no program, no leaflet, no printed matter at all, no membership cards, not even a miserable rubber stamp, only obvious good faith and good intentions." He joined a few days after they invited him.

He was thirty when he joined the Worker's Party, and was committed to making it succeed. There were only seven members in the German Worker's Party and Hitler was hell bent on expanding. He made fliers and sent invitations. They even posted an advertisement in a local anti-Semitic newspaper. After the ad, Hitler insisted on moving to a bigger venue and they did. About a hundred people showed up to this meeting, and Hitler was to address a crowd for the first time. Here is how Hitler described the experience in his book, *Mein Kampf*: "I spoke for thirty minutes, and what before I had simply felt within me, without in any way knowing it, was now proved by reality: I could speak! After thirty minutes the people in the small room were electrified and the enthusiasm was first expressed by the fact that my appeal to the self-sacrifice of those present led to the donation of three hundred marks."

They used that money to print more advertisements for future meeting with Hitler as its featured speaker. Hitler ranted about the Treaty of Versailles and blamed the Jews for all of the problems that Germany suffered under. Slowly, attendance began to rise and numbered in the hundreds.

Before I continue, I'd like to point out that Hitler didn't invent anti-Semitism, nor did he dupe people into believing that the Jews were the cause of German problems. Imagine for a moment that the man pictured using marks as wallpaper is in America, and those aren't marks, they're dollars. The government is in disarray; there are riots, strikes, and constant political assassinations and uprisings. Also, New York City was occupied by Mexico because the government wasn't paying its bills. The Germans weren't evil, they were scared people. Blaming things that they don't understand on those that are different from them is something that human beings do a lot.

I'm not attempting to excuse the behavior, but it wasn't Hitler that "caused" the anti-Semitism. Jews dominated banking back then. That's not to say all Jews were bankers. It's the same as saying blacks dominate basketball in America, but all blacks can't play basketball. To say that you were anti-Semitic was almost synonymous to saying you were against capitalism. One of the notable assassinations was the German Foreign Minister Walter Rathenau, a Jew, in 1922. Hitler simply tapped into an already existing anti-Semitic fervor in the country. It should be noted that it was the Weimar Republic itself that was to blame for the economic woes of Germany.

Hitler was nominated the leader of the Worker's Party and he urged the group to hold its first public meeting. Some people in the committee were against it because they knew that the communists would interrupt the meeting. Hitler said it was an opportunity to distinguish the party from the communists who were actively fighting the military. The public meeting went ahead and communists did disrupt Hitler during his speech. He simply continued speaking over the communists, as the crowds cheered him on, and he eventually drowned out the communists.

By 1920, the party began to get recognition. Hitler decided on two new things. First, they needed a symbol: the Swastika. Hitler didn't invent it, but he saw it before at other anti-Semitic gatherings. Secondly, he wanted people to readily identify the party with National Socialism. So they added national and socialism to the name of the group. The group was then called the National Socialist German Workers' Party, or Nationalsozialistische Deutsche Arbeiterpartei in German. The shorthand for this name was Nazi.

The Nazi party grew in popularity as the hyper-inflation got worse, but when the currency began to stabilize, the people no longer looked to Hitler to vent their anger for them. It was a long ten years of trying to gain traction and failing. It wasn't until the Great Depression of 1929 that the people wanted to hear the vengeful tirades of Hitler again. The catastrophic deflation was exactly what Hitler needed for his message to be taken seriously. In 1930, many Nazi party members were elected to office. In 1932, Hitler ran for president and won.

The chaos that ensued thereafter doesn't concern me for the purposes of this book. The circumstances that opened the door for such a man are what interest me. Hitler wasn't at all unique and the Germans aren't evil. Given the same set of circumstances, how do you think you'd fare? What would you do to protect your family? You are super self-righteous? How would you feel if bread cost a million dollars one day, and you only had 900K on you? Then a few years later, that same loaf of bread only costs $10 but you had no money? America would never commit genocide? Too late, that happened already. So did slavery and a whole host of other things. I want to impress upon you that the very same thing could happen here, again.

Caesura - My Turning Point

I apologize, dear reader. I have brought you thus far and have ultimately decided on a detour. Everything was going as planned. I put forth a simple thesis that wealth can be created by the simple action of exchanging hands. I started out this work by sharing with you the inevitable demise of our society by something as simple as the driverless car. I honestly struggled to start with that, as I wished that to be in the end. For a few weeks I mulled over what I should include or exclude, and whether or not I should end by sharing how it was I imagined these things that I'm writing.

The concept was quite simple. Look at American history through the lens of the flow of wealth. I limited myself to about 70K words, as I'd like ordinary people to read this book, understand it, and not be intimidated. Coming close to the end, I struggled to decide the period of time that mattered the most, in terms of the flow of wealth.

FDR was clearly a significant character. It is quite entertaining to discover all that he tried to turn this nation around. I wanted to share a little more about his scuffles with the Supreme Court, and how he ultimately reconciled with them. After this came the "Second

New Deal." Some of the things that FDR accomplished during his tenure still exists, but Republicans were always against them. To this day Republicans seem fixated on dismantling FDR's social programs, regardless of the consequences. With or without the social programs, the New Deal didn't "rescue" the American economy. Some historians say that the Great Depression lasted only ten years, but others say it lasted until WWII. Socialists argue that the massive government spending project called WWII was what turned the nation around. I partly agree, but I believe it was mostly that people of color had slowly become an integral part of the economy.

Then there is Hitler. I wanted to tie Hitler to other great leaders, in that he arose during a time of economic depression and delivered on his promise to turn the economy around. America had FDR and Germany chose Hitler. The world likes to demonize Hitler, but he is one of us. He is a shade of humanity that exists, and waits in the shadows for his time. Under the banner of unity and pride, the weak are attacked. Hitler, like those who came before him, was a genius. He was a brilliant orator, seasoned military tactician, and fervent in his beliefs. Unfortunately, he was a brutal mass murderer.

I wanted to talk more about the "Civil Rights Movement." The same deflationary seeds that allowed men like Hitler and FDR to rise to power, were the very same for Martin Luther King. The only difference was that the extreme deflation was isolated to people of color in America. King and Hitler shared similar traits, but obviously there were differences. King seized upon the energy of the people and begged for peace. Calling it the "Civil Rights Movement" ultimately betrays the moment in time our nation passed through. We may never know what a blessing we had with King — ever.

Consider what happened to the nation after the assassination of MLK. A wave of riots spread around the country, known as the "Holy Week Uprising." Other than the Civil War, the country has never faced that level of civil unrest. Riots broke out in 110 cities all around the country. The Federal Government was preparing for an insurrection. On April 4, 1968, King was assassinated. On April 5, President Lyndon Johnson ordered a mobilization of the Army and the National Guard. The Civil Rights Act of 1968 was rushed through Congress. People wonder why marches aren't as effective now as they were back then. I can tell you, quite simply, the nation was on the brink of another civil war. King's "protests" were stopping the insurrection.

I don't wish to marginalize people and events in history, but my time is limited and I can't betray why I'm writing in the first place. I write for my own sanity. I've trapped myself within myself, and refused to share what makes me beautiful. This is my third book now. The first, *Violent Tremors: Journey to Overcome the Legacy of Slavery*, was poorly written and way too long. It was over five hundred pages, even after I cut two hundred pages. I didn't consider myself a writer at that point, but I was at the end of my rope. I had tried every type of therapy, and the only thing that I'd succeeded in doing, after almost ten years of effort, was to stop my panic attacks. I decided to write down all the things that I've kept secret and share it. It really isn't a good book, though I lifted entire passages and added them here.

Writing that book felt good, even though it sucked ass. It took almost two years of typing and crying, but it was worth it. Part of me wanted to write this book next, but I didn't want to write another serious book. I needed an emotional break. So I wrote *Why Women Cheat: Confessions of a Pickup Artist*. I believe this book is better than my first book, and my plan to get radio interviews went off without a hitch. What I didn't like were the interviews themselves. I felt dirty after almost every one. Eventually, I stopped returning people's calls and taking interviews. The book was called *Why Women Cheat*, not *How to Make a Woman Cheat*. I'm not interested in breaking stereotypes about pickup artists; I have enough stereotypes to deal with already.

Here we are, at this moment in time. I'm brought back to the reason I write, and the ultimate purpose of this book. I write because it gives me a chance to express myself, and I want to change the world with this book. With that, I must thrust this book into the present, as the present demands my focus. History is important, especially when looked at in a different way. But my very essence demands that this book change direction with the clarion call, "I Hate the Police!"

SOLO MIO – IF I HAD MY WAY

A Challenge to Black Activists and Leaders

Our Hidden History

It is a bit frustrating to have had to do my own personal study of the series of events regarding people of color, in order for me to learn about the truth. The Martin Luther King in history books and portrayed by prominent activists isn't who he actually was. Let's consider the actual moment in history. There was a brutal suppression and oppression of people of color in the US. The oppression was state-sponsored and varied in severity across the nation. In the 1930s and '40s, many people of color traveled to India to learn directly from Gandhi how the Indians overcame the oppressive rule of the British Empire.

Mohandas Gandhi was an Indian activist and wanted to free the nation of India from British rule. He recognized the factors at play and devised a tactic to thwart the British power in India. The British Salt Acts prohibited Indians from making or selling salt. They were forced to buy salt from the British, including a hefty salt tax. Gandhi reasoned that if enough people break a foolish law nonviolently, the law couldn't punish everyone. In addition, the violent reaction of the police force to nonviolent protesters would shame the people in charge.

Gandhi started the Salt March that took place from March to April 1930. First, he wrote a letter to British Viceroy Lord Irwin, stating his intentions. Gandhi didn't bother waiting for a reply. On March 12, Gandhi left his ashram in Sabermanti with a few of his followers. It was the beginning of his 240 mile journey to the sea. Along the way he spoke to large crowds about the oppressive and unfair rule. Gandhi expected to be imprisoned or beaten, but the British feared nationalist backlash and allowed the march. By the time he reached the ocean, many thousands of people were following Gandhi. Even though the police crushed the salt deposits into the mud, Gandhi picked up the mud and began making salt. The law had been broken.

Almost 80,000 people were arrested for making their own salt from the ocean, including Gandhi. Even without Gandhi at the helm, millions of people would go to the sea and gather salt water in order to make their own salt. Eventually, the police became frustrated and began to viciously beat the peaceful demonstrators. The news of this sparked an international outcry, and the British Empire began to soften its stance on salt. That small defeat led to larger ones, and eventually the British ceded control of India back to the Indians.

MLK was a constructed persona modeled after Gandhi. When King returned to America, he became a holy man just as Gandhi was. If the US weren't mostly Christian, I doubt King would have become a Christian minister. King was a revolutionary. He was highly intelligent and clearly he could move a crowd. Everything he did was planned. The famous march from Selma to Montgomery had a clear objective and laser-like focus. It was a mirror image of Gandhi's march, except it was only a 50 mile march. The point was to dramatize openly unfair laws, nonviolently, and win public support. King's actions and the violent reactions did create lasting changes. For this I am grateful.

This is not what concerns me about black activists today. It's the total disregard for who that man was and from whence he came. A short time ago, after harassment by the police, I felt helpless and enraged. I didn't know what to do, so I contacted the NAACP for the first time in my life. After emailing back and forth a few times with the VP of the NAACP of the Brooklyn chapter, I was still so angry I began to scream out of frustration. I then searched the internet for the Black Lives Matter movement. I wanted to go someplace and shout my heart out. After I clicked the search button, I recalled hearing the phrase "a riot is the language of the unheard." This phrase is oft repeated, in the media in response to protests and riots, by black pundits.

I looked up the full quote, and this is what King said, "It is not enough for me to stand before you tonight and condemn riots. It would be morally irresponsible for me to do that without, at the same time, condemning the contingent, intolerable conditions that exist in our society. These conditions are the things that cause individuals to feel that they have no other alternative than to engage in violent rebellions to get attention. And I must say tonight that a riot is the language of the unheard."[24]

What angered me even more than police abuse was the frequent misquoting of King. How many times have black "leaders" gone into communities that are rioting and misquoted King? MLK was a revolutionary in every sense of the word. Nonviolence was a strategy for change that he employed successfully. To be clear, it was all staged. The incident with Rosa Parks was staged, the marches were staged, the entire King persona was staged. He had a clear vision of what he wanted and dramatized the story he wished to be told. The picture that I'd been given was not who he was.

Moreover, it seems that no one wants me to know about all of the riots that took place all around the nation during King's time. People of color were arming themselves and readying for a revolution. I'm pissed that I've never heard of the Holy Week Uprising. Why is this not in any history books? You mean to say the time when black people openly rebelled in 110 cities isn't worthy to mention? The only military occupation of the nation, besides the Civil War, doesn't count as useful information? There were many other open rebellions as well. They were called "riots" for some reason. When King spoke of riots and rebellions, what was he talking about?

In 1964, people of color "rioted" in a number of cities in New York State. They are called the "Harlem Riots" even though the rioting spread far beyond Harlem. Governor Nelson Rockefeller had to mobilize the National Guard to quell the violence. In 1965, blacks in South Central California "rioted" for six days straight. Governor Pat Brown mobilized the National Guard to quell the violence. Forty-three "riots" took place during the summer of 1966. They lasted twenty days and took place in Cleveland; New York; Philadelphia; Chicago; Jacksonville, Florida; and South Bend, Indiana. The "riots" in 1967 were far worse than the rest. The "riots" spread from coast to coast and from city to city. Even the small cities were rocked by black "riots." Of course the National Guard were called again. In Newark, many people died as the National Guard began shooting indiscriminately into Newark housing projects. The "riot" in Detroit was so intense that the National Guard was no help.

---

[24] Speech by MLK entitled "The Other America" March 14, 1968

Governor George Romney asked President Johnson for help and Federal Troops were sent in.

People like to say that the Holy Week Uprisings were caused by the death of MLK, but I respectfully disagree. The violent pushback against white oppression was already underway. If there is any doubt to this, President Johnson put together a commission to figure out the causes of the civil disorders and to give recommendations to the President, Congress, governors, and mayors on how to prevent or contain future disorders. It was called the Kerner Commission because it was chaired by Otto Kerner, the Governor of Illinois. The Commission's report was handed to the President on March 2, 1968, a month before MLK's assassination.

The Commission detailed the grim reality of racism in the country. It predicted more and potentially larger rebellions. It warned that continued white racism would lead to cities under martial law and recommended that the country find a way to integrate blacks into American life. The report asserts, "White racism is essentially responsible for the explosive situation, which has been accumulating in our cities since the end of World War II. Pervasive discrimination and segregation in employment, education and housing have resulted in the continuing exclusion of great numbers of Negroes from the benefits of economic progress... What white Americans have never fully understood but what the Negro can never forget–is that white society is deeply implicated in the ghetto. White institutions created it, white institutions maintain it, and white society condones it."

In respect to the police, the report states, "The police are not merely a 'spark' factor. To some Negroes police have come to symbolize white power, white racism and white repression. And the fact is that many police do reflect and express these white attitudes. The atmosphere of hostility and cynicism is reinforced by a widespread belief among Negroes in the existence of police brutality and in a 'double standard' of justice and protection—one for Negroes and one for whites." This report is still highly relevant today. The 1968 report commented on black youths like this, "A new mood has sprung up among Negroes, particularly among the young, in which self-esteem and enhanced racial pride are replacing apathy and submission to 'the system.' " It is the same today with the Black Lives Matters activists.

After the Civil Rights Act of 1964 was signed into law, President

Johnson is quoted saying, "We just delivered the South to the Republican Party for a long time to come."[25] The Democratic coalition that started with FDR, was being split apart by black civil unrest. People of color at this time consistently voted Republican. Yet the Kerner Report was a bridge too far for white America, at every level. President Johnson never publicly acknowledged the report, and was privately upset that the report failed to mention any of his initiatives to make black lives better. Vice President Humphrey did speak about the report, stating that it "overstressed the racism angle...I wish some of the energy of the rioting had gone into self-improvement... (Black people should be) lifting themselves up by their own bootstraps."[26] Richard Nixon, then a Presidential candidate, comments on the report, stating it "in effect blames everybody for the riots except the perpetrators."[27] Nixon ran on a platform of "Restoring Law and Order." The nation wasn't ready to hear that white racism was what bothered black people. Nixon won the Presidency and in 1970 passed the Controlled Substances Act, then declared a "War on Drugs."

Consequently, a follow-up study was commissioned, entitled "One Year Later." This second report was as discouraging as the first report was, concluding, "The nation's response has been perilously inadequate. The nation has merely come one year closer to being 'two societies, one black and one white, separate and unequal.' "

It was bad enough that I've been insulted, threatened, and lied to by the police. It's far more distressing to me that I never knew any of this. Part of me thinks that it was providence that led that police officer to harass me to the point of protest. Otherwise, I would've never decided to study the history of the police myself. I would've also never known about an actual uprising of people of color in the US. I'm disgusted by the people who call themselves black leaders. How could I never know of any of this? I clearly understand why white people in this country would wish to forget this period of history, but how can black leaders not see the chain of events as they happened and not make sure that I personally would never forget?

---

25 "Second Thoughts: Reflections on the Great Society," New Perspectives Quarterly 4, Bill Moyers
26 Daily Illini, March 26, 1968
27 The Times-News, March 4, 1968

The people who call themselves black leaders, say that they are emulating Dr. King, when in fact they are not. Looking at black activism, after MLK, I can say that there is no discernible planning. Now that I know about the Holy Week Uprising, it is all clear. Black activism has devolved into causing civil disobedience and then demanding concessions.

I can't express to you enough how upset I feel that I didn't know about the actual black revolution. Is it my fault for not knowing? Who should I blame? Who should I trust? Part of me doesn't even believe any of this happened given how the entire country is so quiet about it.

We Need to Accept Racists and Fight Discrimination

Who am I to judge black activists? I understand their frustrations and sympathize with them. I'm a nobody. Up until this point in my life, all of my battles were inside. Writing has helped me tremendously in that department. Though I am a nobody, haven't you noticed that the shape of racism and discrimination has changed? It is clear to see that after the Holy Week Uprising, the country was set on jailing as many people who look like me as possible. They were careful to make sure any overt racism was not present, so that people like you couldn't make a media moment over it. Moreover, MLK's original strategy of non-violent resistance is pointless as well, as there are no overtly biased rules that are uniformly applied to everyone. I'm personally vexed by the "rallies" activist have held at the slightest hint of racism.

Let me tell you something. There are no combinations of words that will make a person who thinks I'm subhuman suddenly change their mind and believe I'm their equal. You cannot fight racism wherever it pops up, as this is and always has been a racist country. The worst part of watching the incessant racist whack-a-mole is the white people apologizing for whatever they said or did. That apology then somehow makes everything better? This is a racist country!

I want you to understand what is actually happening, and why you should be concerned about the future. What white people are going through today is no different from what homosexuals went through fifty years ago. Homosexuals in the past were afraid and ashamed to say what they think and feel, because of a potential public backlash. Whites today who say what they actually believe or feel could lose their jobs in the same way homosexuals could lose their jobs in the past and the present in some places.

If I were a white man, I'd be terrified right now. I would be concerned that people would treat me as I treated them in the past. And I'd be right! On the one hand, it's nice to see that people of color have some power in this country. But tell me, what is the difference in being fired for being gay or being fired for being a racist? Most jobs don't require homosexual sex or racism. So why should it be okay for a company to not wish to associate with either? Just because one is more socially acceptable? I'm troubled when I hear black activists say "good riddance" when a white person loses their livelihood over something racist that they said in private. I have even heard, on a number of occasions, "We just need to wait for them to die." As if racism will die with the previous generation.

What you have succeeded in doing is putting an entire nation of white people in the closet about their views on race. Do you not see that you have become the very thing that you claim to be fighting? It's as if you are fighting for the right to discriminate in the same way whites have. What is the end goal? That people see things your way? Then you should expect a revolt by whites. Public shaming of whites because of racism isn't what MLK did; he shamed unjust laws and practices.

It bothers me that people all around the country are demanding that the Confederate flag be taken down. This country is littered with our racist past given that this is and has been a racist country. It's a waste of time to name all the places historical racists occupy our country. But if you take issue with the Confederate flag, look in your pocket and find a non-racist president on your money. If black activists continue down the road of shaming whites for even the slightest hints of racism, then the "riots" that speak the voices of the unheard will be that of white people.

I would be in favor of laws protecting racists from retribution, because I'm against discrimination, not racism. Where do we draw the line if we continue to attack "racists?" Should we then attack the Chinese for having negative views of the Japanese? How about attacking a Pakistani for their views about Indians? There are many such divides around the world, and definitely present in NYC. We have to accept that this is a racist country just as much as racists have to accept that it is a black, Latino, and gay country. I would be proud of black activists for fighting for a racist's right to be racist, but not to discriminate. With so many people of color languishing in jail, the fight shouldn't be about who said "nigger" in private. I could care less how many white people said nigger, as long as they let my people go.

Though I am nobody, and I am alone, I do have a plan of action. It was great fortune that my latest police harassment took place in the midst of me writing this book. I needed a change in direction. But before I lay out my plan, there are other things that I need to explain.

Reparations Nazi II – Sorry Mr. Coates, Still No Reparations for You!

There is this recurring theme, among Democrats, that the Clinton administration's policies were incredibly amazing for our economy. While I think President Clinton is a great politician, I disagree with the premise. Politicos fascinate me. They always like to look at an event or a moment in time and pick out the things that would further their agenda to focus on. If the Clinton ideas were so amazing, why aren't Democrats talking about all the things that produced the huge budget surplus that happened during the Clinton era? Don't get me wrong, I'm sure that there are some great things that he did. I'm just not aware of them. The things that come to mind about the Clinton presidency don't strike me as positive. It is at the very least debatable whether or not the Clinton policies had any effect on the economy.

Why was there a budget surplus? You should know by now, at least if you've been paying attention. Especially since we are talking about reparations again. Women fighting their way into the economic fabric of the US is what created the financial boom during the Clinton era. He simply claimed credit for it. Hillary Clinton had more to do with the economic surplus than Bill Clinton did. There are two things to address: First, why women shouldn't get reparations, and second, how did women entering the workforce make the nation wealthy?

They seem like two separate questions but in fact both are answered by financial reciprocity. While it is true that people of color were actual slaves, there existed another class of people that were quasi-slaves: women. Women weren't allowed to work and were essentially the property of men. A while ago, I made the case that slavery in America actually cost white Americans money. Also, that before the '60s, America was a third world country. To be honest, I have no way to prove these statements. I simply imagined it was this way, since I understand how money works.

Q: What would happen if all people of color and women willingly agreed to the pay that they received, adjusted for inflation, before 1960?

A: The answer to this question allowed me to posit that America was a third world country. In truth, people of color aren't as big of a block as women are. If sixty percent of our population were forbidden to work or were severely underemployed, then we would be suffering from crippling economic stagnation. Literally, trillions of dollars' worth of economic activity would simply evaporate.

It was great fortune for Bill Clinton that feminism was making its most productive push just as he entered office. Rebecca Walker, a writer, coined the term "third-wave feminism" in 1992, and Clinton officially took office in 1993. This "third-wave" is considered to have continued into the present day by most feminists. It was also good fortune that Hillary Clinton was in the White House, bucking the tradition of being the President's arm candy.

While it could be fun and interesting discussing all of the breakthroughs women made during the Clinton era, alas, I don't have the space for it. But from my own experience, I remember in my youth a hoopla about an episode of *Murphy Brown*. The show was already controversial because Murphy was an independent and strong woman. I never watched the show because I never got the political references. But I made sure to watch the show when she had a baby as a single mother. By today's standards, that show would be tame. But I remember it being a huge controversy back then. It was during the Clinton years that women reclaimed their identities and came out from under the shadow of white male supremacy.

Q: Why shouldn't women get reparations?

A: There are many ways to answer that question, but to be consistent with what I've said in this book, women not working made men poor. Women not working made the entire country poor. I challenge anyone to show me the economic benefit of keeping women from working.

Moreover, it makes even less sense that women regularly get paid less than men. It is literally economic suicide. Having any group of people consistently making less money than others actually costs the entire economy money! Women fighting their way into the workplace multiplied the wealth, thus adding to the budget.

How Would I Do It Locally?

If I were Governor of New York, and I had legislative support, I would change the way we operate our economy. Given that there are a number of federal laws prohibiting certain actions, I would need to proceed carefully. It would be beyond vital for me to utilize the multiplicative power of inflation and the divisive power of deflation in tandem to create a successful economic environment. It isn't enough to tax and spend, or cut taxes and cut spending. Both of those things are exclusively inflationary or deflationary.

The first step would be to set up a statewide collective, like the NRA in the FDR era. The main difference would be that my NRA would be voluntary. Let's call it the National Reciprocity Collective (NRC). Businesses can choose to join the NRC, and if they do, they will be required to:

- Allow the NRC to track their banking information.
- Promise to spend 70% (adjustable) of every dollar they made to taxes, employees living in partner states, or other NRC registered businesses.
- Be subject to an additional tax if spending requirements aren't met given a certain time period.

Q: Why would you want to track financial transactions?

A: It would give the quants I hire further data to look at. Inflation and deflation have the power to destroy an entire civilization. I honestly don't think the information would be as adequate as the information you would get from analyzing all the data from the IRS, but it is better than nothing. With this data I would be able to get a good understanding on how much the state economy would inflate or deflate given different policy actions.

Q: Why bother explaining the rest? Why on earth would any businesses voluntarily submit to these rules?

A: I understand your concern, but the other points are important too. Well, all right. It's simple, actually. I understand that wealth can be multiplied by it exchanging hands multiple times within the same community. It's first important to set up a mechanism that would multiply the wealth for me: the NRC. Businesses will rush to sign up for the NRC because I will promise to pump money into the NRC mechanism.

I would start with seniors, for example. Once the NRC is operational, I would petition the Federal Government to allow me to manage Social Security payments to the seniors in New York State. Then I'd give seniors in New York the choice of receiving their SS payments as scheduled, or to get the NRC augmented SS payment. If they decide to keep their payments the same, then nothing changes, except they will receive checks from the State rather than the SS office. If they decide to get the augmented payments, I would double whatever Social Security paid them with conditions. Instead of getting a check to be cashed, they would get an NRC debit card. Thirty percent can be spent in any way the seniors chose. If they want cash, they can withdraw or transfer that money. But seventy percent, or whatever percentage I choose, can only be spent at NRC approved vendors.

You may be wondering where I would get the money to double SS payments for seniors. Either I can use a surplus, spending cut, tax increase, or I can simply borrow the money. The point is, the money itself will multiply, and the hope is that the multiplication directly benefits New Yorkers. Also, seniors deserve a raise! Let's consider how such a thing will likely work.

The first businesses that will likely line up to get some of this new money are rental companies. There are scores of real estate investment companies that incorporate out of state to avoid taxes. Moreover, the wealth garnered from rental properties in New York often leaves the state. Seniors all around the state will be looking for apartments with the NRC logo. Given that the NRC is voluntary, this new money won't have an immediate impact on rental prices. Some people may have "exclusive" NRC rentals, and attempt to raise the price. Some seniors may fall for this, but there are many properties in the state. Competition from non-NRC rentals should stabilize prices.

Also, some seniors may look to become homeowners. This would lead to similar results. Seniors would be looking for home loans that are NRC approved. In both cases, the money exchanges hands in New York at least three times. First to the senior, then to the rental company or bank, and finally to the place that the rental company or bank spends.

Let's consider this. Of every dollar, about seventy cents will be spent in New York. I know this isn't entirely accurate, but please stay with me. Fifty cents of that dollar comes from the Federal Government. About 10% of every dollar made enters the state coffers, approximately. This means that about seven cents will be paid in taxes by the rental company, and about five cents will be paid in state taxes for the person or business where the rental company spent its money. So technically, the giant increase given to seniors only costs thirty-eight cents, but not fifty cents per dollar. This is if, and only if, the money stops exchanging hands after the third iteration. With each new iteration, the raise for seniors could potentially drop to zero. In fact, it might make the state money.

Q: Why seventy percent?

A: It's just a number. I have no idea what number would be the best. The actual number should be flexible. Meaning, sometimes it might be good for it to be 83% of every dollar and sometimes it could be good for it to be 47% of every dollar. Too much inflation or deflation will hurt the state economy. Being able to control the multiplication of the money in this way is important.

Another way the money can be multiplied is by increasing the rates at which the money exchanges hands. For example, I could give a three week time limit for the seniors to spend the money or it evaporates. The three week timeframe could be increased to three months as well. The timeframe for spending the money received can also be added to the entire NRC program. Decreasing the amount of time the money can be held will rapidly increase the amount of wealth in the local economy. This, in tandem with a steep penalty for not achieving spending goals, will make the economy move.

Q: How does this utilize both inflation and deflation?

A: This is quite simple actually: choice. Most large companies will probably set up shell corporations to handle NRC transactions. For example, seniors may want to get a cell phone. Verizon Wireless, seeing an opportunity with NRC, signs up and puts the NRC sign outside its local stores. Verizon might use accounting tricks to show that they are spending "x" amount of dollars locally. The problem that they will face is, should they charge different prices for NRC customers?

Of course there will be a law forbidding transaction fees for NRC customers. If that's the case, there is no way to charge a higher price to NRC customers. First, because the NRC customers have a choice of where to spend and what class of money they want to spend. Two-tiered pricing wouldn't work. I will utilize capitalism's destructive nature to my advantage. Since everything is voluntary and people can make their own choices, capitalism will check the inflation of the NRC.

Q: Will you stop at seniors?

A: Absolutely not! I will one by one give raises to every public servant in the state, even the police. The raise won't be as high as the raise for seniors though. For example, I could start with fire fighters and increase their wages by thirty percent. The fire fighters will be given the same choice seniors were given. In this way, the state node increases its reciprocity with other nodes in the state by a huge factor. I would only increase wages as the budget increases.

There is another factor at play as well. If NRC businesses can remain competitive with other businesses, ordinary New Yorkers would feel proud buying NRC, knowing that the money would be spent locally. While not perfect, it at least addresses the destructive deflationary effects of unchecked capitalism.

Q: You said something about partners? What is that?

A: The NRC won't be exclusive to New York; any state or government can join. States and other nations will be given a multiplier based on its reciprocity to New York. This multiplier is similar to the multiplier I spoke of on the federal level. But individual companies, located anywhere, can also apply to the NRC. The money sent to those out-of-state companies, from New Yorkers, will be tracked and they would owe New Yorkers some spending. It would be up to that individual company to buy NRC.

Q: Won't you alienate states and countries?

A: Yes, and hallelujah! These places believe that slave labor is the way to prosperity, and are simply places were money goes to die. There will still be a place for them in the New York economy, but an ancillary one. Their role is to make sure prices don't go up too much. They can get mad all they want, but they don't spend their money in New York, or places with great reciprocity to New York.

I wouldn't attempt such a thing in a small state that is dependent on other states for survival. A potential boycott could be an issue. New York State can itself be self-sustaining. Also, the wealth created in this way will be constantly looking for new partners. If companies don't exist that won't adjust to this new way of doing things, potential profits will create those companies.

The Day that I Realized that I was an American

While I'm not going to spend any time on the Obama presidency, I think it's important and relevant the experience that I had during his presidency. I admit that I refused to vote for most of my life. I actually planned not to vote in 2008. I'm very stubborn and I had already made up my mind that politics had nothing to do with me. I did wind up voting, but not because of the obvious reasons. In 2008, I was at a point in my life where I thought that I had to date as many girls as I could to see if there was one I'd like to keep forever. That didn't really work out as planned, and I wrote a book about it. The other issue is that honesty is my highest value. While I'd be out meeting new women, they invariably would ask who I was voting for. "I'm not going to vote" was a surefire way of getting women to walk away from me. It was very frustrating being in NYC when everyone suddenly had become super political.

I honestly voted just to tell women that I did vote. It came down to two choices, grumpy old white guy or young, attractive black guy. Being in NYC, there was no way that I could vote for McCain. Doing that would be a guaranteed way of not dating for months. So, I didn't vote for Obama because he was black. I voted for him because the women I find attractive voted for him.

I wasn't paying much attention to politics at the time. But I began to pay attention after he got elected and the vitriol coming from the Republicans was unprecedented. I didn't pay attention because they were mistreating the first black president poorly. I paid attention because the things they were saying about him, were said about me at some point in my life. I felt a solidarity with him, and it was strange.

When I realized that dating lots of women didn't change anything, I essentially had given up everything. I had struggled many years, fighting for my own sanity. I gave up and dropped everything, spending five and half months sitting by a Dominican beach watching the waves come and go. When I returned, a lot had changed, including my interest in politics. I watched all that I could on all the 24-hour news networks.

I remember September 2012, because that's when the four dead Americans were shipped back home after the attacks in Benghazi. I watched the event on television, because something inside told me that news was important. Usually I'm blank and empty inside, and the pageantry for the dead Americans didn't change that. It didn't register to me that people were sad or that their speeches were somber. I simply laid on the couch and blankly stared at the television, because I knew it was important.

At one point, Obama and Clinton reached out and held each other's hand. I sat up and clasped the center of my chest with my hand. It was rare for me to feel anything, but I was overcome with an emotion and I had to analyze what had happened. The following was my internal thought process.

"What is this feeling? I feel good. Why am I feeling this? Ummm, because the President and Hilary like me? I know they like me. Wait, that's selfish. This memorial for four dead Americans…why would that have anything to do with me? Obama and Clinton care deeply for Americans, and I'm an American. I'm an American? I am an American!"

This may not seem significant to some, but for me that was a profound moment. I was 34 years old and I never believed that I was fully an American until that moment. Even though I never said it out loud, I knew that I was a second class citizen. I believed that if America had a choice, she would send me somewhere else. It took a black president, a female Secretary of State, and four dead diplomats for me to realize that I am a real American.

I don't think I'm ready to wrap myself up in the flag, or get teary eyed when I hear the national anthem, but I'm comfortable now saying that I'm an American citizen.

The History of the Police

The Basic Elements

It is in my nature to think of solutions to challenging problems. Thus far, within the context of the change in direction in this book, I've laid the groundwork for what I wish to happen and also tied up the threads that existed before the change. Even with all of this, it is essential to enumerate the essential elements that make the police what they are today. In addition, I need to clarify "hate." Being the emotionally incomplete person that I am, I may not truly appreciate what actual hate is. But whenever I see a police officer, negative emotions well up inside of me. I cannot recall favorable memories of the police. In the last twenty years, most of the times I thought I was going to die, I was surrounded by police. Almost all of the hateful things said to me, other than by family members, were by the police.

The truth is, the police know how I feel about them. They know how the community that I live in feels about them. Some of you reading this might be confused. How can a man without a criminal record have such negative feelings towards the police? If you really are confused, let me give you a suggestion. Find a person of color and ask them a simple question: "Would you rather share a meal with a table of armed police officers or ex-cons?"

Obviously, I would choose to eat with the ex-cons. Why? First, and most importantly, the ex-cons know that they can't get away with anything. The difference between the two groups, to me, is one group can rob, kill, harass, insult, or ruin me and get away with it.

The other group will never get the benefit of doubt. I don't trust the police and try to avoid them as much as possible. The police clearly know how I feel, and they don't care. Police work can't take place when the people they serve don't trust them. What the police care about are their self-elevated statuses and the ability to get away with whatever they choose. Also, I would feel comfortable at a table of ex-cons as I know many ex-cons, and they are good, down to earth people that the world has cast aside. I have immediate family members in jail and in the penal system. I don't want to know the police. They disgust me.

Some of these things we have touched on, but not expressly, regarding the police. Here are the historical elements that created the modern police:

- Guns
- White-Male Supremacy
- Slavery
- Socialism
- Technology

Early Policing

As we discussed in the beginning, the colonies had no formal structure and the crown allowed them to govern themselves. Also, in the beginning, everyone was an indentured servant. These servants were all called to defend the settlements from rival empires and hostile natives. Thus, all of the servants were called upon to act as guards of the settlements. These individuals were the police, the army, the judges, and the jury. It is important to recognize that this was the germ of all of American policing.

We also discussed the uprisings in the 1600s. After the Tidewater Aristocracy declared blacks subhuman, we can solidify that the essence of American policing was "a white man with a gun was the law." Blacks were forbidden to marry, carry arms, and so on. Granted, this job was an unpaid job, but was still vitally important. It was likely required that all white men be armed, in case of an emergency. Free market capitalism at its finest. Get people to work for free!

There were no formal laws, and no formal law enforcement. Whatever a white man with a gun said was the law, was in fact the law.

When two white men disagreed about "law," the only way to settle it was a gun duel. These duels are often dramatized in our movies, and usually reference the "Wild West." People continued to duel for hundreds of years in America. Even though we had constructed an elaborate justice system. I'll simply relay two of the most famous duels in American history.

The first is the duel between Alexander Hamilton and Aaron Burr in 1804. At the time, Hamilton was the former Secretary of the Treasury and Burr was the sitting Vice President under Thomas Jefferson. The two men were fierce rivals. Apparently, Hamilton was saying bad things about Burr and Burr challenged Hamilton to a duel to "restore his honor." Burr won the duel, was tried for murder and acquitted. The next duel was between Andrew Jackson and Charles Dickinson in 1806. This duel took place more than twenty years before Jackson became president. Jackson didn't like that Dickinson insulted his wife and he challenged him to a duel. Dickinson was a prominent lawyer at the time. Clearly, Jackson won by murdering him. Jackson was said to have participated in several duels in his lifetime.

What do these two examples illustrate? That the law of the land was a white man with a gun. Even with an entire legal system set up by the Constitution, taking the law into your own hands was still the way things worked. Do you not know why? The police didn't exist. In fact, during the time of those two duels, the army didn't exist. Who would you call if there was a problem? Back then, all of the states/colonies existed with a town crier. The town crier was an unpaid job and usually rotated among the white men. The town crier's job was to warn white men with guns if there were any problems. If there were escaped slaves, hostile natives, or invading armies, the town criers would cry. The most famous town crier was John Revere.

The Slave Patrol

In the North, the colonies organized volunteer groups known as the "Night Watch." It wasn't enough to have a single town crier. Male residents were required to volunteer some of their time to watch the towns at night. They were to watch for hostile natives, fires, thieves, and runaway slaves. In the event something happened, they were supposed to alert other white men with guns.

In the South, a similar system arose, except they had an additional concern: a slave rebellion. In 1704, South Carolina instituted the first slave patrol. Other Southern colonies quickly followed suit. The slave patrol was supposed to assume the same duties as the northern Night Watch, with the added work of patrolling the domiciles of the slaves and catching runaways.

There was a real problem with the slave patrol — nobody wanted to do it. It was seen as a free service for the wealthy slave owners. The slave patrol had become a derogatory term to whites in the South. They called the slave patrol patty rollers or paddy rollers, a derivative of "patroller."

In 1757, Georgia made it a law that all white men were required to serve as a paddy roller. People could hire others to patrol in their place, but if they didn't show up to patrol, they would be fined. This again put the burden of the slaves on non-slave-owners. The result was that the slave patrol wasn't organized nor did they care much about what they were doing. Things changed dramatically in the states after news of the Haitian slave rebellion of 1791 circulated. The slave patrols became more vigilant, but in 1819 the first paid slave patrol came into existence in Savannah City, Georgia.

Paddy rollers received a dollar for every night they patrolled, and the entire patrol shared the reward for catching escaped slaves. This was the very first paid, organized policing agency in the country. Other cities and states followed suit. It is important to reiterate that a white man with a gun was in fact the law of the land. There was no need for a day watch as white men were usually awake during the day.

When the Town Criers Lost their Jobs

A problem arose in Northern colonies in the early 1800s that the watchmen of the time couldn't seem to handle. Riots began to break out all over. The Southern colonies didn't have these riots, for reasons we discussed previously. Looking at each riot individually, we can accept the reasoning that historians want us to believe. But looking at them together, we get a different picture. Here are some of the bloody riots that took place:

- The Cincinnati riots of 1829
- New York City Anti-abolitionist riot of 1834

- Boston's Gentleman's riot of 1835
- Cincinnati Riots of 1836
- New York City Flour riots of 1837
- Philadelphia Nativist riot of 1844
- New York City Astor Place riot of 1849

There were many more riots, long before the Civil War broke out. These riots, and others, had a variety of "causes." Some were about immigrants. Some were about freed slaves. Some were about abolitionists. I would like to suggest to you that the issue at hand was technology. The nineteenth century was rife with riots and rebellions, but the eighteenth had almost none. I already suggested before that the steam powered boat irrevocably changed the US.

The steam powered boat was invented in 1807, and in the years to come people no longer needed to indenture themselves in order to get to America. It took about a week to traverse the Atlantic, in time. The civil unrest, in my opinion, was the violent end to the practice of indentured servitude. White men in the North were afraid of losing their jobs to immigrants or freed slaves and began lashing out.

The only force able to stop the riots was the army. Large cities in the North then created twenty-four hour police departments. First was Philadelphia in 1833, then Boston in 1838, followed by New York City in 1844. These police departments were modeled after British police force inspired by Sir Robert Peel. The tenets of policing put forth by Peel seem reasonable, and the Americans copied them. The main difference between the American and British police is that the American white man used to be the only law of the land, and the American people needed to understand that the police were above the common man. Otherwise, no one would respect them. This belief that the police are above the common man still exists today. In fact, the police go out of their way to demonstrate that they are above the common man.

The Civil War and Beyond

Since slavery was technically outlawed, there was no longer a need for the slave patrol. Most of the old slave patrols simply changed their names to police stations. We spoke about the KKK, but I didn't talk about its disbandment or its multiple resurgences. The Klan was a volunteer organization to maintain the social order. After reconstruction, the Klan disbanded once the former slaves were back on the cotton fields. The Klan resurged in the 1930s as blacks were being expelled from the cotton farms during the Great Depression. They resurged again in the '60s when the blacks were completely expunged from cotton farming. The Klan of the '60s remains until this day, as the blacks never returned to cotton. The Klan wasn't a radical organization on the fringes, it was a mechanism of social order and is a part of the history of policing in America.

In 1850, a former NYC police officer founded his own private investigation firm, the Pinkerton National Detective Agency. Allan Pinkerton became famous for allegedly foiling a plot on the newly elected President Lincoln. Pinkerton and his agency were then hired to protect the president during the Civil War. The Pinkertons were the first agency to ever defend a sitting president. Later that job would be handled by the Secret Service.

The Pinkertons are definitely a part of police history considering that people would often call the Pinkertons before calling the police. In fact, by the 1890s, the Pinkertons had more active agents than the entire army. If there was something important that needed defending, the Pinkertons were hired. If there was an important crime that needed investigating, the Pinkertons were called. The Pinkertons had the largest database of mugshots and fingerprints in the country. The Pinkertons were hired to catch outlaws and bank robbers. Also, there are a number of famous movies about the Pinkertons.

The police were afraid that the Pinkertons would simply take over, as the people regarded the Pinkertons as the only competent police force in the nation. There was even the Anti-Pinkerton Act of 1893, due to fears of the private company's influence. The Pinkertons were even outlawed in a few states. Nonetheless, the Pinkertons were the go-to police force for capitalists. They were hired to infiltrate and break up unions all around the country. The Pinkerton Agency is now a subsidiary of Securitas AB.

The Modern Police Force

What we call the "police" today is radically different to what people in the past considered them. This nation, as you know, was founded by the principles of pure capitalism. During the Great Depression, the people revolted against capitalism and elected a socialist president, FDR. We spoke of the things FDR did to combat the Great Depression.

The riots in the early twentieth century are far too numerous to bother enumerating. All of the "causes" are just as numerous. There was extreme poverty and civil unrest, and the President was a socialist. He didn't bother calling the Pinkertons. Instead, he put many thousands of people to work as police officers. Hence we have a giant organization of individuals who are called to be above the common man, paid for by the government.

It is quite telling that self-proclaimed free market capitalists are constantly attacking the socialist institutions that FDR created. Yet they don't bother attacking the police. It is a fact that we didn't have a giant police force before FDR. You can't say that we can't privatize the police as we had a history of a mammoth private police force in the Pinkertons. The modern police force is a combination of the early colonial law in one's own hands ideology and the power of socialism.

So, to clarify the change in the police during the FDR era: As people of color were being expelled from sharecropping and gravitating to cities in the North, large-scale riots began to break out. This was white people rioting against black people moving into their neighborhoods. The National Guard were called most of the times to quell the violence. The police force was expanded in order to stop the rioting.

Slavery

Apart from the Slave Patrol, what did the police have to do with slavery? After the Civil War had ended and the thirteenth amendment was ratified, southern whites looked for a way to enslave the recently freed colored people. It was an entire community effort. Though the KKK existed, it wasn't enough. A new system of slavery was established to replace the old version. Sharecropping was invented to keep the black population in the place the nation thought they belonged.

Sharecropping seemed fair on the surface. The sharecropper would share in the profits of the sale of cotton with the landowner. The only problem was that most of the year, the sharecropper didn't have enough money to feed their families. To compensate, sharecroppers were offered loans with up to 90% interest. These things were bad enough, but the sharecroppers were often cheated and abused by the landowner, and no police agency was there to aid or assist.

There was no escaping sharecropping. You'd think that people could just pack up and go someplace better, but this is where the "police" came in. Unattended Negroes were a problem. I can just hear the phrase often uttered to me shouted at people who are trying to escape, "*Where are you going?*" and "*What are you doing?*" If the police discovered that you were trying to leave your sharecropping farm, they would drag you back and you would be punished by the police, the KKK, or the land owner.

There were still many blacks who refused to sharecrop. This is where the new Vagrancy Laws and Black Codes came into play. Vagrancy is the condition of an individual who is idle, has no visible means of support, and travels from place to place without working. It was up to law enforcement to decide who was vagrant and who wasn't. It was simply another way of controlling the recently freed slaves. Here is an excerpt from Mississippi's Black Code:

> *That all freedmen, free negroes and mulattoes in this State, over the age of eighteen years, found on the second Monday in January, 1866, or thereafter, without lawful employment or business, or found unlawfully assembling themselves together, either in the day or night time, and all white persons so assembling themselves with freedmen, free negroes or mulattoes, or usually associating with freedmen, free negroes or mulattoes, on terms of equality, or living in adultery or fornication with a freed woman, free negro or mulatto, shall be deemed vagrants, and on conviction thereof shall be fined in a sum not exceeding, in the case of a freedman, free negro, or mulatto, fifty dollars, and a white man two hundred dollars, and imprisoned, at the discretion of the court, the free negro not exceeding ten days, and the white man not exceeding six months.*

The 13th Amendment is stated as follows: "Neither slavery nor involuntary servitude, except as a punishment for crime whereof the party shall have been duly convicted, shall exist within the United States, or any place subject to their jurisdiction." It was a simple matter of convicting colored people of crimes, then sentencing them to slavery. The Convict-Lease system was instituted just after the slaves were freed. Whenever someone wanted to hire slaves, the police would simply go on the hunt and arrest black people who weren't sharecroppers. After the Civil War there was a rapid spike of crime, on paper.

The Convict-Lease system was worse for people of color than actual slavery, as the slave owners of old had a vested interest in keeping the slave alive. In the Convict-Lease system, the person leasing the convict paid the state a small fee and they could do whatever they wanted to with the prisoners. Many were worked or beaten to death. It didn't matter because you could always just lease another convict. Whenever a new project was to start, crime would spike, and lots of young black men were arrested and convicted within a 24-hour period. These convicts built railroads, paved roads, mined coal, picked cotton, and anything else you wished them to do.

This was all very legal, if and only if no one verified the evidence against these young men. But there was another form of slavery that cropped up after the Civil War: peonage. Peonage was expressly forbidden in the US, but no one was ever prosecuted for it. One man was prosecuted for murdering his peons, but not only for the crime of enslaving people. He was convicted of murdering an unknown amount of slaves. I didn't write his name or the amount of people authorities think he killed. It angers me too much that the only way you could be prosecuted for catching random people from the street and making them your slave, was if you brutally murdered more than a dozen of them.

Peonage is the system where an employer compels r any place subject to their jurisdiction a worker to work, in order to pay off a debt. The police helped individuals who wanted full time slaves catch black people and force them into peonage. The Convict-Lease system was only for a period of months to years, but peonage was essentially for life. The police would simply round up people of color, who weren't sharecroppers, and say that they owed a person money and they needed to pay. Then they were sent to court and summarily convicted of owing a debt. Then the people of color were forced to sign an agreement of servitude for a period of time, in order to pay off the debt. Unfortunately, most people were never freed.

There is some debate as to when peonage and convict-leasing ended. The convict-lease system became unpopular due to bad press over the numerous murders and deaths, and it slowly went away. Peonage ended when WWII began. After the Japanese bombed Pearl Harbor, FDR looked over the next logical place they would attack. He was concerned about a revolt among the people of color and attempted to correct peonage, though he didn't touch the sharecropping system. The directive from his Attorney General, Francis Biddle, was called Circular No. 3591. Though convict-leasing still happened, there was less of it. Though peonage was no more, it was all for the war effort… so as to not risk a Negro rebellion in the midst of the war.

The Revolution and More Slavery

As we discussed, sharecropping didn't end because of kind-hearted white people, it ended because the cotton picker was invented. All of the systems of control, meant to direct blacks into manual labor, were inadequate to deal with the masses of people ejected from the cotton industry after this invention. Even if they could, where would they direct the people of color to?

Blacks began to migrate to large cities across the nation. The police were used to corral them into designated areas. Banks and public policy helped as well. But the most visible arm of the government was the police. People of color faced brutality and harsh economic conditions all around the nation, and this was a recipe for a revolution. Riots broke out all across the country and the police weren't equipped to deal with them. The National Guard and the army were called in all around the nation and even in the capital.

Once Nixon was elected, a "War on Drugs" was declared. There are conspiracies about the CIA putting drugs into communities of color. I can't confirm any of this. But rest assured, before the Nixon administration, there was no drug problem. The more the nation fought this "War on Drugs," the bigger the "problem" of drugs became.

Eventually the War of Drugs was replaced with "War on Crime." Our prison system is now full of men of color. We now have more people in prison than any other nation in the world. That is only mostly true. If you look at the thirteenth amendment again, you'll see that we actually have one of the world's largest slave forces. Thousands of companies in America use prison slave labor. They can't unionize or complain and they are paid pennies to nothing per hour. There are literally hundreds to thousands of companies that utilize prison labor. No point in listing them all. Just to give you the breadth of what prisoners make in America, I simply copied and pasted what UNICOR offers directly from their website, at www.unicor.gov.

1. ADP & Telecommunications Services
2. ADP Entry Services
3. ADP/Modular Furniture
4. Agricultural Products
5. Air Filters
6. Aircraft Cable/Harness Assemblies
7. Amplifiers
8. Animals Raised for food
9. Antennas & Related Mounting Accessories
10. Architectural Signage, Interior & Exterior
11. Armament Training Devices
12. Armor, Personal (helmets & vests)
13. Assembly/Packaging
14. Awards & Plaques, Custom (M)
15. Badges & Insignias
16. Bags
17. Bags & Sacks
18. Bags, Flyers' Helmet Bags
19. Bar Code Labels
20. Baskets, Inserts, Canvas
21. Baskets, Laundry, Postal Service
22. Bathmats
23. Battery Box
24. Battery Box Assemblies
25. Battery Equipment
26. Battery, Non-Rechargeable
27. Bed Ladders
28. Bed Sheets
29. Beds
30. Bedspreads

31. Beef
32. Beef Cattle
33. Binders, Screen Printed!!!!
34. Blankets
35. Bookcases
36. Bookracks
37. Bookshelves
38. Boots & Transitions
39. Box Springs
40. Boxer Shorts
41. Building Components (steel doors & frames)
42. Building Materials Kit Assembly
43. Buildings, Portable
44. Cabinets
45. Cabinets (storage, wardrobe, vanity, stationery, wall vanity; metal & wood)
46. Cable Assemblies
47. Cable Assemblies, Wire Harnesses, Remanufactured
48. Cable, Cord, Wire Assemblies & Harnesses
49. Cafeteria Furniture
50. Calendar Frames
51. Calendars
52. Call Centers
53. Cantilever Racks
54. Canvas Inserts
55. Cart Inserts
56. Carts
57. Case, Ammunition
58. Case, Radio Carrying
59. Case, Small Arms Ammunition
60. Cases, Flag
61. Casters
62. Catalog/Content Management
63. Catwalks
64. CD Rom (Data Conversion)
65. Chairs
66. Chairs
67. Chests, 4-drawer

68. Circuit Card/Board Assemblies
69. Clocks
70. Clothing, Special Purpose
71. Coats
72. Coats
73. Coats, Camouflage
74. Columnar Pads
75. Communications Equipment, Miscellaneous
76. Computer Furniture
77. Computer Recycling Activities
78. Connectors, Electrical
79. Contact Center/CRM Support
80. Container Repair Services
81. Conversion
82. Conveyor Systems
83. Coveralls
84. Covers, Camouflage
85. Credenzas, 4-door
86. CRM Support
87. Cubicle Furniture, Inmate Units
88. Curtains, Berth
89. Curtains, Cubicle
90. Dairy Products
91. Data Capture Services
92. Data Conversion Services
93. Data Encoding
94. Decals (Decalcomania)
95. Desk Trays
96. Desks
97. Digitizing Services
98. Direct Mail Services
99. Distribution Services
100. Document Conversion
101. Doilies/Dish Towels
102. Dollies
103. Doors, Steel Security
104. Dormitory Furniture (Metal) & Mattresses (M)
105. Draperies

106. Drop Cloths
107. Duty Belt
108. E-Commerce Support Services
109. E-Government Support Services
110. Electric Lamps, Table & Floor
111. Electric Power Distribution Cables
112. Electric Wire & Power Distribution Equipment Repair
113. Electrical & Electronic Properties, Measuring and Testing Equipment
114. Electrical Components
115. Electrical Connectors
116. Electrical Devices, Miscellaneous
117. Electrical Equipment & Components, Repair & Rebuilding
118. Electrical Leads & Harness Assemblies
119. Electrical, Portable & Hand Lighting Equipment
120. Electronic Equipment Recycling
121. Embroidery Services
122. Engine Electrical System Components/Cable Assemblies
123. Engine Rebuild & Repair
124. Engine, Electrical Systems Components, Repair & Rebuilding
125. Engineering & Design
126. Envelopes
127. Equipment Repair & Maintenance
128. Equipment, Individual
129. Ergonomic Seating
130. Extension Cords, Electrical
131. Exterior Signs
132. Extreme Cold Weather System Jackets
133. Extreme Cold Weather System Trousers
134. Eyeglasses, Non-Prescription
135. Eyeglasses, Prescription
136. Face Shields
137. Fences, Security, and Temporary
138. Fiber Optic Cable Assemblies & Harnesses
139. File Cabinets
140. Filters
141. Floodlights
142. Folders, Printed

143. Food Preparation & Serving Equipment
144. Footlockers
145. Forest Service Posters
146. Forms, Printed, Multipart, Carbonized & NCR, Standard & Custom
147. Fulfillment Services
148. Furniture, Metal & Wood; Office (M); Dormitory (Metal) (C); Modular & Stand Alone
149. Generators, Generator Sets
150. Glasses, Non-Prescription
151. Glasses, Prescription
152. Gloves, Glove Inserts
153. Goggles
154. Gowns
155. Gowns, Hospital
156. Graph Paper
157. Grounding Cable Assemblies
158. Guided Missile Components & Support Equipment
159. Guided Missile Propulsion Equipment
160. Hazardous Materials Markings
161. Helmets
162. Help Desk Suppor
163. Hinges, Metal, Various Sizes
164. Hospital Gowns
165. Household & Quarters Furniture (Metal)
166. HTML Tagging
167. HVAC Filters
168. Imaging & Indexing
169. Individual Equipment
170. Industrial Racks
171. Inmate Admission Kits
172. Interior Signs
173. Isolators
174. Jackets
175. Jumpsuits
176. Kit Assembly & Packaging
177. Kitchen Equipment & Appliances
178. Kitchen Utensils

179. Labels and Tags, Printed
180. Lamps
181. Laundry & Postal Carts
182. Laundry Services
183. Letters, Die-Cut
184. License Plates
185. Light Kits/Fixtures
186. Lights, LED
187. Lights, LED Turnkey Solutions
188. Live Animals, Raised for Food
189. Lockers
190. LRM Support
191. Mail Bags
192. Mail Satchels, Repair
193. Mailing Services
194. Mailroom Furniture
195. Map Shelving
196. Markings
197. Materials Handling Equipment
198. Materials Handling Equipment Repair
199. Mattress Covers
200. Mattresses
201. Meat
202. Mezzanine Systems
203. Milk
204. Mirrors
205. Mobile Utility Carts
206. Modular Computer Furniture
207. Name Plate Holders
208. Name Plates
209. Name Tags
210. Napkins, Fabric
211. Neck Gaiter
212. Newsletters/Periodicals, Printed
213. Night Vision Equipment, Emitted & Reflected Radiation
214. Night Wear
215. Nightstands
216. Nightwear & Underwear, Men's

217. Office Furniture
218. Optical Character Recognition (OCR) Services
219. Optical Equipment
220. Outerwear, Men's
221. Outerwear, Women's
222. Overhead Storage
223. Packaged Furniture, Packaged Office Solution, Packaged Office Program, Turnkey Packaged Furnishings (Consistent with GSA Schedule)
224. Pads, Columnar Printed
225. Pajamas
226. Pallet Racking
227. Pallet Stacking Racks
228. Parachutes, Meteorological
229. Partitions, Acoustical
230. PC Reuse/Demanufacture
231. Pillowcases
232. Planters/Wastebaskets
233. Plaques, Award (M)
234. Plastic Tableware (cup and tray)
235. Plastic Tableware (fork, spoon and knife)
236. Posters, Offset and Screen Printed
237. Portable Buildings
238. Power Distribution Systems
239. Prefabricated Structures
240. Prescription Eyewear
241. Printer Stands
242. Printing
243. Promotional Products (M)
244. Protective Caps
245. Protective Clothing
246. Publication Distribution Services
247. Radio Carrying Case
248. Radio Mounts
249. Recreation Signs
250. Recycling Activities
251. Remanufactured Appliances
252. Remanufactured Cable Assemblies

253. Repair & Rebuild Vehicular Equipment Components
254. Reproduction Services
255. Restocking Services
256. Rigid Wall Shelters
257. Robes
258. Routed Signs
259. Safety Equipment, Goggles, Spectacles, Face Shields
260. Safety Signs & Decals
261. Scanning
262. Screen Printing, Textiles
263. Seating
264. Security Camera Cable Assemblies
265. Security Doors, Metal
266. Seismic Racking
267. Settees
268. SGML Tagging
269. Sheets
270. Shelters, Rigid Wall
271. Shelving
272. Shirts, Men's
273. Shirts, Men's (Long & Short Sleeve)
274. Shirts, Women's
275. Shoes (Distribution)
276. Shorts, Athletic
277. Shredders, paper
278. Signs
279. Slotted Angles for Storage Units
280. Small Arms Ammunition Case
281. Sofas
282. Solar Panels
283. Solar Systems Maintenance, Repair and Rebuilding
284. Speakers, Speaker Boxes & Related Accessories
285. Specialized Shipping & Storage Containers, Repair Service
286. Stack Supports
287. Stationery, Printed
288. Stools
289. Storage Aids
290. Storage Systems

291. Storage Units, Modular
292. Structural Shapes, Iron & Steel
293. Structures, Prefabricated
294. Sweats, Shirts & Pants
295. Swim Trunks
296. Switches
297. Systems Furniture
298. T-Shirts
299. Tablecloths
300. Tables
301. Tables
302. Tack Boards
303. Tags, Identification
304. Tarpaulins
305. Telephone & Field Interview Services
306. Terry Cloth
307. Testing Equipment Kit Assembly
308. Testing Services
309. Text Processing
310. Textile Repairs
311. Time Measuring Equipment
312. Tire Racks
313. Tool Bags & Hardware Boxes
314. Tool Kit Assembly
315. Tool Kits, Packaging & Distribution
316. Towels, Bath, Dish and Hand
317. Traffic Signs
318. Transitions and Boots
319. Trousers
320. Trousers, Camouflage
321. Trousers, Surgical
322. Trousers, Utility
323. Trunks
324. Turtlenecks, Mock
325. Typewriter Stands
326. Undershirts

327. Uniforms
328. Utility Carts, Mobile
329. Vehicle Racks
330. Vehicular Components, Miscellaneous
331. Vehicular Components, Remanufactured
332. Vehicular Equipment Components, Repair & Rebuilding
333. Vests, Body Armor
334. Wall Art
335. Wall Shelters
336. Wardrobes
337. Washcloths
338. Waste Receptacles
339. Wastebaskets
340. Wheeled Vehicle Replacement Parts
341. Wire Assemblies, Miscellaneous
342. Wire Bundle Assemblies
343. Wire Rope Assembly
344. Wiring Harnesses
345. Word Processing Services
346. Work Clothing
347. Workbenches
348. Workstations, Pre-Wired
349. XML Tagging

This, by the way, isn't the only organization in America employing prison slave labor. Slavery has come a long way since the shameful convict lease system. Now they are on the internet trying to show the lighter side of slavery. You can buy direct from UNICOR or a place like PrisonBlues.net. The Angola Prison complex, in Louisiana, itself was a plantation before the Civil War. After the Civil War they began to house prisoners and went back to farm work. Prisoners in Angola still farm to this day. Also, it isn't at all racist that this plantation was named after the area in Africa where the majority of the slaves were purchased to work there.

The reality is that there is a demand for slave labor and the police are filling that demand with arrests. These arrests and convictions usually involve people who look like me. Thus we are here in the present.

A Moment of Personal Action

The Point of Ingress

Recognition of the moving parts is just the first step. Next is making a clearly defined goal. *"I want to repay the police officers the kindness that they've shown me."* There is a challenge there. First, there is the Police Bill of Rights. Next, the police are the only agency that I can use to get any type of redress. I could attempt a civil action, but this will cost me a significant amount of money. This is just the beginning.

There are a multitude of problems with the justice system in America. Although crime keeps going down, incarceration rates keep going up. Public defenders are always overwhelmed with cases and usually recommend that people take a plea deal. The District Attorneys rarely prosecute police with crimes. And so on.

My interactions with the police have forced me to act; thus, I'm an activist. I must act, or else I'd feel helpless and powerless, and I'm not. Thus, it is clear and obvious what is driving our entire system of justice: slavery. There is no point in protesting police injustice, the police bill of rights, unfair sentencing, or anything else. Slavery is the driving force.

Making the Impossible Possible

It's possible that you've come to this book from my website, www. stopnyslavery.com, but if not I'm going to explain to you the function of it. First, there will be a video of me on a green screen sharing the continuity of slavery from the 1600s up until now, and I will ask for the viewers to make a personal commitment to end slavery.

Next is my personal lobbying effort to the legislators in New York. I will post the response from legislators to my lobbying about slavery in New York. While this may not seem like much, it is an important step. I would like to know who is for or against slavery in my state. I ask these politicians if they would support legislation banning slavery in all forms, including in prisons, in New York State. Also, I ask them to ban people, businesses, or local governments from profiting from the incarceration of inmates. I will post their replies for all New Yorkers to see.

The last and most important step is to create a social network geared towards prison slaves. The problem that many people in my shoes face, is that most people don't know that slavery still exists. I will ask people who care about this issue to share my video and site with their social networks. Then ask the people they know if they are or were in prison. Next, those individuals will post a picture, how long they worked as a slave, how much money they made, what happened if they refused to work, and so on. It is my hope that such a thing would go viral and shed a bright light on the human side of current American slavery.

Will This Work?

It is my hope that through the combination of sharing historical context, political pressure, and a viral shaming of American slavery, we can collapse the entire system. This is because the system cannot survive without slavery. In fact, I should say more accurately, the system of slavery cannot exist without slavery.

I don't really know how effective such a strategy will be, and I'm quite honestly afraid. I'm worried that I will be personally attacked for trying to upset the "order" of things. Nonetheless, I must press on. I'm now committed. If I fail, I will try something different. I'm a citizen and a human being, and I'm not helpless.

HOW TO DESTROY AMERICA

Prologue

First, I'd like to say that this isn't how I wanted to end this book, but it was a nagging reality that I have held for many months now. Let me tell you how I thought I would end this book. I wanted to tie together the rise and fall of the British Empire, with the very same mistakes the US has done. The revolt that the British Empire experienced was a corporate revolt. In the same way the British Empire installed corporations around the world to represent its interests, the US did the very same thing after WWII. It seemed like a fitting end, especially since I started with "Driverless Cars will Destroy America!"

The truth is, I'm a secretive man and this entire book reflects a challenge that I had given myself well over 15 years ago. I recounted for you the moments that I received two phone book sized documents from the Federal Reserve. What I didn't tell you is that it pushed me over the edge and I had a breakdown. When I realized what the Fed had sent me, I also realized that most of the far right wing stuff that I was reading was all garbage. I had spent a number of months praying and fasting, hoping God would change me in some way. I was angry, frustrated, alone, and depressed. Whenever I was in such a state, I would think of something impossible to remain sane. I remember being curled in a ball, on the floor, when I asked myself, "How could I destroy America?"

For weeks, I remained on the floor curled in a ball. Sometimes I used the bathroom and returned to the floor. Rarely, I would eat. Most of the times that I got up from the floor were to check the feasibility of my plan of attack on the internet. Before this exercise, I knew literally nothing about how our government worked. After this exercise, I understood quite a bit, as most of my plans of attack simply wouldn't work. For well over a year, I wracked my brain trying to destroy the nation. After I had come up with a solution, I decided to return to civilized life. Figuring out how to destroy the country seemed to help me with my personal problems. But I still had a long way to go from there.

Being a secretive person, I shared the plan to destroy the nation with no one. The reason I struggled with including this section was, again, my secretive nature. The reality is this: This book was written to stop my plan to destroy the US. I understood the weak points and tried to shore them up as much as possible. Clearly understanding the point of attack led me to look for historical references to bolster the plans to destroy the country, and to defeat my plan to destroy the country. I'm absolutely not a historian, and before writing this book there were many things that I was unaware of.

Part of me was concerned that I would be picking and choosing historical events out of context. I was beyond surprised that our history lines up so completely with my plans and premises. I had no idea about Greenwood, the Civil War, Martin Luther King, the New Deal, slavery, and on and on. America has had, and continues to have, the same weaknesses that can be exploited. These weaknesses can be avoided, however, if people take the threats posed seriously.

What prompted me to finish the book this way? The police! Part of me is concerned about people taking my plans and adopting them for themselves. But I'm sick and tired of being treated as a second class citizen. I'm still angry, and I don't care what happens. If someone looks at my plans and decides to act on them, I want to make something clear. I didn't create the weaknesses that exist in America. It's not my fault that these weaknesses can be exploited. If all you can do is blame me for America's weaknesses, then I say you are lazy and stupid.

The Weakness and My Original Plan

I believe that I was twenty-two years old when I originated this plan. The point of ingress should be obvious if you have read this book up until now. If I were planning to bring this country down, I would attack the flow of wealth in the nation. The weakest points in this flow of wealth are the very rich. But there are other choke points within the flow of wealth that can also be exploited. Back then I chose to attack the health care system.

It is a fact that health care spending accounted for 17.4% of the US GDP in 2013.[28] It is expected that health care spending will reach 19.6% by 2024.[29] These numbers should be mind-numbingly alarming. These numbers are barring a health crisis or epidemic. Think about this, in a few short years, if nothing calamitous happens, twenty cents of every dollar spent in America will be spent on health care! There are many terrorists out there hoping to strike a decisive blow against the US, why not attack the health care industry?

The health care industry itself is a financial choke point in the flow of wealth in the nation. There are others that are bit more difficult to affect, but for now let's focus on health care. Here is what you should be most concerned with. Of the money sent into the healthcare industry, where is that money spent? How much of it is spent? And how quickly is it spent? The problem with so much of the nation's wealth passing through the hands of a few people, is that those people can effectively shape the course of the nation's future.

Can you imagine that there are places in the nation where wealth passing through the health care industry will never reach? Then it isn't hyperbole saying that the **Health Care Industry is making certain parts of this nation poor**. This is not asking whether or not these areas have insurance. The germ of the original plan was to simply increase health care spending. I reasoned that dramatically increasing health care costs would have an immediate impact on certain areas, creating relative deflation zones.

I didn't need to go any further with my reasoning back then. If I could find a way to get the nation to sharply increase their health care spending, it would create sharp enough imbalances to collapse the economy. I know that I haven't yet convinced some of you. I simply wanted to convey the germ of the argument. The truth is, I was incredibly naive back then. I didn't believe that race played a significant enough factor to cause any change. I've had sixteen years to ponder these matters, and I'm of a different opinion now.

---

[28] Report by the Centers for Medicare and Medicaid in 2014
[29] National Health Expenditure Data: NHE Fact Sheet 2014

Destroying America Step by Step

Identifying the Goals

If I were going to destroy this country, I would need to be clear on my targets. The primary target would be the very rich. It would be my primary goal to keep them from spending any money in the US. They are in fact the weakest link in the nation's flow of wealth. Money flows to them effortlessly, and they don't have to spend most of it to survive.

Next are the flow of wealth choke points. The one we discussed is health care, but there are many others. Creating a comprehensive attack on all of the choke points is unnecessary and risky. I would get caught easily if I tried to be too broad. Also, this is not a blueprint to follow and actually destroy America. It is my hope that people will look at this and make changes. Anyhow, the other choke points are fairly obvious.

Lastly, there are the minority groups that I would need to hurt by the subsequent deflation. People in the nation love to openly proclaim that, "We solved our race problems back then." I can tell you that not much has been "solved." If I could, I would use women as the group, but honestly it seems too challenging to make the hated group all women.

Tying all of these things together are the "cyclical downturns" in the economy. People call this cyclical because it happens regularly. Even though it happens regularly, doesn't mean that it's normal. What is happening is the destruction of wealth. If market forces are allowed to operate, wealth will flow in one direction until the wealth stops flowing. In the midst of one of these regular downturns, is the perfect time to strike.

Create a Boogeyman and then Attack

I've been debating which groups that I wish to use to blame the attacks on. So I'll have all three. I will use a masked Mexican, an Arab, and an African American to claim responsibility for the things that my group will do. I would use current issues relevant to those specific groups as demands. It's important to recognize that I would choose things that are incredibly hard to achieve. For example, the Mexican demand could be to take down the existing wall along the US-Mexican border. I would use current events to find causes to take up.

The point of using front people to make masked video demands, is to create a solidarity with those specific groups. People will likely disagree with our tactics, but will agree with the causes. These are the groups that will be most hurt by a decrease in the flow of wealth. Especially African Americans. The saying is, that African Americans are last hired and first fired. As long as I've been alive, this has been true. It is good fortune that white Americans openly claim that there are no race relation problems in this nation. The denials would be used to our advantage, with propaganda. One last piece is that we will likely only use white Americans to carry out any of our plans. The minorities will just be the face of the group.

While this group will be clearly defined as a "terror" organization, mass deaths or highly valued targets won't be important. If deaths do occur, we will either denounce them or not claim responsibility. We need to make sure the minorities aren't turned off by inhumane actions. Solidarity needs to be the initial aim. Although, things may not turn out well for the minorities as a whole. Now that we have a front organization, let's implement the original plan and see what happens.

The Sketchy Original Plan

In order to make the original plan a success, we would need an airborne, contagious virus that could be deadly without medical attention. What comes to mind is something similar to the H1N1 virus in 2009. I'm clearly not a virologist, so all I could do is wish for such a thing. If money weren't an issue, I would have my swine flu-type virus. What's unfortunate about the H1N1 virus is that a vaccine is currently available.

At this point, I must admit that my plans would likely be exposed. This is because there are very few people in the world who could provide me with such a virus. In order for this plan to work, I would need to have incredibly deep pockets and have many friends in high places. If you assume that I'm capable of having such a virus, then the plan can go ahead.

My group would post a video on the dark web, and spam the news media of its existence. The message will be in English, Spanish, and Arabic. It would warn of an imminent attack on the US because of (fill in the blank) reasons. If only America would do (fill in the blank), then there would be no attacks. It is important to declare intentions first and then follow through; this way, future bluffs can be taken seriously.

If I have the means to acquire the perfect virus, then I would have a simple means of dispersal. I would have white members of my organization disperse the virus in high traffic areas in white parts of the country. I would target train stations, malls, concerts, and airports. It is necessary to get maximum exposure. Also, to keep deaths to a minimum, the authorities will be alerted within, say, 48 hours. The warning time would depend on the speed at which the virus propagates. Though deaths may occur, that isn't the goal.

It's important to warn the authorities to try and save the infected. The first issue is that there is a limited amount of space at hospitals. The CDC can lend a helping hand, but care will literally be stretched to the limit. When I first thought this scenario up, there was no Affordable Health Care Act. Now that more people have health care coverage, the rate of health care spending won't jump as dramatically as I'd hoped. Yet it still will be an issue.

You may be wondering why I'm attacking average white Americans? In the long term, the racial divisions will come into play. This is an attack on the very wealthy in the nation. You see, usually during an economic downturn, the wealthy put their wealth in a variety of health care stocks. They are known as defensive assets. This is because the health care industry, as a standard, does their billing one year after health spending took place. Increasing the amount of people accessing care will spook investors who would otherwise invest in healthcare stocks without thinking. In fact, people may sell health care stocks in the sight of a nationwide epidemic. In the midst of an economic downturn, this type of thing could lead to a catastrophic deflationary event.

I hope the catastrophic event doesn't happen yet, as we still have more planned. Health insurance companies will need to increase premiums or they will go out of business. Although I did intentionally attack white Americans, it will be the minorities who suffer economically. The higher premiums will affect them the most, as they make the least in the country. Again, the ACA may have put a damper on this as well. Markets are fast moving, if the government doesn't allow insurance companies to raise rates, then the government will need to step in and increase its spending on health care.

A financial collapse would be a great outcome. But increased spending to the insurance companies is also a good outcome. The question is this, if the government sharply increases its spending, and that spending passes over minority groups, doesn't that make them more poor? The fact is, there is a limit to how much of the nation's GDP the health care industry can take up before there is a catastrophic collapse.

I admit that this plan isn't all that great. There are far too many things that I would have to assume. But the essence of the plan still remains solid. Redirect the wealth away from certain areas, and get the government to increase its spending.

Plan Revised – Attack the Money

The first part of the plan can take place, or not. If it is possible to have the perfect virus and not get caught, I would use it. But more realistically, if I were to try and destroy the country, I would need to go low tech. There are a multitude of arteries in this country to attack, and most of them are low priority and unguarded. Before I talk about a real plan, let's again try something that will likely not work.

In 2003, there was a blackout in the Northeast part of America. I remember that day because I was at the movies for a matinee, and everything went black. It took me an hour to walk home. According to the Anderson Economic Group, the US lost $6.4 billion dollars in that blackout.[30] Since then, the threat of a terrorist group causing a blackout of that scale has been a constant reality.

I wouldn't want to do something like this for our group. First, because it hurts everyone uniformly. Next, it cripples the economy for only a short period of time. Investors can be sure that in a few days, things will return to normal. Also, if the blackout period is extended for a very long period, people with lots of money will utilize their massive wealth to take advantage of the situation. It wouldn't help my goals at all.

In addition to this, exposed transmission lines, substations, and transformers aren't really that exposed. I would need a detailed layout of the nation's grid and someone highly skilled in order to tell me which points to attack. Also, I would need to attack during peak hours, likely in the summertime for maximum effect. This is because there are subsystems and people constantly monitoring the grid for fluctuations. There can't be a cascade failure if the other grids aren't also overloaded. Next, the so-called exposed locations are far too exposed. The odds of coordinating a simultaneous attack during peak hours at various spots in the country and not getting discovered is slim. Plus, the fact that there needs to be precise timing means that if one person is caught, everyone

---

[30] AEG Working Paper 2003-2, Patrick L. Anderson

is caught. There is a lot of fear-mongering about this subject, but I wouldn't worry too much about it.

Why bother mentioning it? I already stated it. The blackout cost America $6.4 billion. Now I want you to ask yourself, how did the blackout cost that much money? If you've been paying attention, most of that money was lost from money not exchanging hands. People couldn't work nor could they purchase goods and services.

The reason I brought this up is to show you how things can swing in either direction. We all know how to cause catastrophic deflation. If enough people stopped spending, money would simply evaporate. Now I want you to think to yourself, what would the opposite of a blackout for a few days be? And can we do the opposite to create $6.4 billion?

An Attack Based in Reality

The best places to attack, that don't require advanced degrees in anything, are the roads, bridges, and railroads. I would include tunnels, except those things usually have some degree of security. The idea is to not get caught, and to encourage, with propaganda, others who aren't in my group to take action on their own. I personally wouldn't use bombs, at least not in the beginning. The only thing that would work are long distance rifles. It would be a dream come true if I could use EMP devices to disable cars and trucks on the road, but that technology isn't currently available.

Though I think guns are appalling, the ubiquity of them in America makes it an easy choice for conducting terror plots. I would instruct my snipers and would-be snippers, through propaganda, to make homemade silencers so that their positions aren't given away as they attack the highways in America. Unlike the electric grid, the road map is available to anyone. The attack would happen at simultaneous locations around the nation. Again, losses of life won't be good, especially in the beginning. We would be aiming for car and truck tires. I would prefer truck tires. Once one car is disabled, it would slow the rest of the traffic down to make shooting the other tires out much easier.

How does creating a traffic jam destroy the country? It is an important first step, but it can absolutely destroy the nation. The biggest problem that America faces is the willful ignorance around what money is and how it actually works. Remember, I would only initiate an attack if and only if the nation was in an economic downturn. This means that the deflationary process is already happening. Attacking high valued targets hoping to get bragging rights is stupid. It is much easier and more manageable to attack over 160K miles of highways with easy to obtain guns.

What does causing traffic jams do? It slows the rate in which money exchanges hands, thus giving the deflation already happening added steam. You may not think this is a big deal, especially if you are a driver. Let me tell you what will happen. My group will cause hellish traffic in dozens of places around the nation. Most if not all of my snipers won't get caught, as snipers are hard to catch. We could use portable sniping stations to get around. We would reiterate our demands for stuff that we would never get. Then the media and public officials would give us the tongue lashing that we so rightly deserve. Sure, some people were a little late for work, but that's all. The public was moderately inconvenienced. The real targets were the trucks, not the cars or the people. Trucks can't take an off-ramp to avoid traffic. There are many places that trucks are banned from traveling. By increasing the travel time for trucks, we succeed in delaying transactions.

Continued delays would raise prices for goods and services in the midst of a spell of deflation. Those areas hardest hit by job loss could potentially see higher prices for goods and services. Given the history of this nation, I'm going to assume those areas are mostly populated by people of color. In addition, the stock market is a double-edged sword. News of even the smallest delays will have an adverse impact on a variety of stocks. If the stock market is already in a tailspin, continuous attacks on the nation's infrastructure would give investors reason to cannibalize the companies listed on the exchange.

Getting caught is a problem. According to the FBI, Washington, DC has the highest ratio of cops to the population. DC has 74.4 police for every ten thousand residents. The Census says we have over 318 million people in America. I'm going to give the police the benefit of the doubt and say that the police ratio of DC is the ratio of the entire nation. This means we have 2.3 million police officers in the nation. The FBI has statistics on the actual number of police, but I want to make it harder for me.

The first problem that the police will be facing is defending the entire 160K miles of highways. In 2002, there was a nationwide manhunt for the "Beltway Sniper." John Allen Muhammad was traveling in a specific area, sending notes to the media, and killing people for three whole weeks, while the entire nation watched. Law enforcement struggled for any leads. After they caught Muhammad, he said, "Can you imagine the damage you could do if you could shoot with a silencer?" It would be just as difficult to catch my group, as they will have solid cover stories, and much better hides than Muhammad. Also, the shootings will be incredibly random so as not to have discernible patterns. In addition to their normal patrols, it will be nearly impossible to protect cars from guns. It's hard enough to protect people from gun violence.

It is important to vary the attacks. This is done to keep a veil of uncertainty around what may happen next. This uncertainty will translate into less investing by those with large sums of cash. The question is, how to vary the attacks? The next easiest thing to do would be to attack bridges that no one cares about. There are scores of structurally unsafe bridges in America. They are the epitome of low hanging fruit for a terrorist organization. I possibly may plant IEDs all around the nation's decrepit bridges long before the sniper spree starts. I would actually warn the police before they go off to find them. Thus adding to our credibility and creating further uncertainty.

Again, it is important to have some level of solidarity with part of the populace. Mass murder might not help us. Finding bombs all around the nation would further increase traffic. In order to make the threats real, I would end all of our propaganda with, "Meet our demands or there will be further escalation." Of course it will take some level of organization and sophistication to pull these things off. But all that's needed is some money, moderate skills, and the will to make it happen.

That would be just the beginning. Making threats and following through gives our group credibility. Further threats will be heeded. Next I would make threats to the nations 233K miles of railroad tracks, and encourage those who have sympathy with our cause to attack the nation's rails. I would warn that there are many IEDs dispersed along tracks in the nation. And I would encourage people to remove rails or plant their own IEDs, "Until our demands are met." The demands will never be met, or at least I'm counting on them not being met.

Protecting the highways is difficult enough, but the rails are a totally different animal. There is no real way to protect them all. Slowing commerce by a small percentage was the goal. This goal is very achievable, with easy to get equipment. This is only the beginning.

Increased Law Enforcement Presence

Calling in the FBI, the National Guard, and giving the police overtime are all expected. These things are paid for by emergency funding from the State or Federal Government. Most of this is paid for by shifting money from one program or project to law enforcement. The rest will be paid by borrowing the money. Hopefully, the investigations are long-lived. What does this do? I created another choke point in the economy. It is a reality that most law enforcement aren't people of color. Either money will be redirected from other areas, or the money will simply be created. This redirection of wealth, even though slight, will have an adverse impact on communities of color.

I'm making assumptions about this nation that some may find disagreeable. This idea that racism no longer exists works in my favor. Even now, some of you are reading this and thinking, How does increasing spending on law enforcement hurt blacks? The real question is this: How much of that increased spending will go to communities of color? Remember, the goal is to stop the people on the top from spending, and also keep wealth from entering communities of color.

Increasing law enforcement budgets are just the beginning. I know that there is no way that law enforcement would actually attempt to patrol all of the roads, bridges, and rails. In all likelihood, they will go to communities of color and be themselves. Current laws already give law enforcement a great deal of leeway in dealing with the public. A terror threat will officially give them a license to step the abuse up a notch.

Again, there are people reading this who think that the police are wonderful angels. My experience is much different from yours. My experience is that they are a lawless gang who can do whatever they want to you and get away with it. I expect law enforcement to overreact and cause problems in communities of color. To reiterate, this is an economic downturn, and many people have lost their jobs. Police escalation will add to the economic uncertainty.

Consider me for a moment. I'm a man without a criminal record and I have no desire to talk to the police or help them in any way. That may come as a surprise to some people. But it is a reality. The police in communities of color are an occupying force whose primary goal is to put the residents in prison (slavery).

You disagree? If a person gets mugged in a white neighborhood, what happens? The person who was mugged calls the police. The police go to the scene and gets a description of the perpetrator. Then they put a "be on the lookout" (BOLO) for that perpetrator, to all police in the area. In white neighborhoods, the police <u>canvass</u> the area asking for witnesses to help the investigation. If the BOLO doesn't work, the police are completely dependent on the information provided by the public. With that information, the mugger is more likely to be caught.

That would be an entirely different scenario in my neighborhood. What would be different? The canvassing. The police don't even bother to canvass in my neighborhood. No one wants to talk to them. Years of mistreatment and harassment have cut the police, in my neighborhood, off from their main policing tool, the public. In my neighborhood, if they don't catch a person running away with the goods, they won't catch him.

This is what makes a terror organization using minorities as front people so appealing. As long as we don't do anything horrific, the public will still be antagonistic to the police. The only tools that they will have available are threats of long prison sentences or large rewards. The threats of prison sentences are a great reason not to interact with police. The only real hope law enforcement has is a large reward leading to our capture. It's my hope that we left no loose ends. In any case, I expect police brutality.

In the Media

It is my great fortune that there exists a medium that will stoke the flames of fear for me. The news will amplify everything we do, and Fox News will make it even better. My terror organization would be a godsend for Fox, as they don't like to cover white homegrown terrorists. If I could, I would hand deliver all of my propaganda to Fox News. If I could manage to get a contagious virus, oh man, that would be the best! Fox News would do all of my work to "other-ize" people of color.

It is my hope that politicians use this moment and try to outdo each other in their response to the attacks. It is my hope that the media and politicians lash out against people of color. They usually do it without provocation. Terrorism will give them the excuse to do "what they all know they need to do." If politicians dare to be measured, I will hand deliver propaganda insulting those measured politicians. Or maybe to fan the flames even further, I could openly insult the most bombastic pundit or politician.

It's important for them to be against the things that we stand for. I want them to openly oppose things that minorities hold dear. In truth, the propaganda part is where I would probably get caught. Unfortunately, it is beyond necessary to play upon the divides that already exist.

What if There is No Crash?

There are far too many unknowns to factor in attacking the American weak points. If there is no crash, then not enough people are being fired, or the rich are still spending too much. However unlikely this scenario is, it needs to be addressed. In this case, investors have something in the economy to be proud of. It would then be my job to make them not be proud of that thing any more.

Here is where I'd need to be flexible. I would spend my time watching CNBC and Bloomberg, and process the commentary thereof. While law enforcement are wasting their time on the roads, bridges, rails, and in communities of color, I will be targeting specific companies or industries. The task facing me is an incredibly simple one: use force to cost a business money.

It is vital to understand that I've been attacking the money the entire time. Targeted attacks on specific companies will have a cascading affect. First, the stock price for that company will falter. In addition to that company's stock price, similar companies and companies that share an index with the targeted company will also see a drop in stock price. In addition, all companies will need to take extra measures to protect their assets. This will cost money, which will further hurt stock prices.

Easy targets are important so that I don't get caught. Claiming responsibility is also vital. I could have a random rotation of attacks between businesses, roads, rails, and bridges. This will continue until the markets go into a tailspin. Hopefully, I'm not caught yet.

Uncle Sam to the Rescue

It has become commonplace for the Federal Government to step in when the economy is in free fall. It will either come from Congress or the Federal Reserve. Trillions of dollars will be pumped into the economy, usually at the last moment. It is important to recognize the directionality of the money spent. Most of this money will pass by communities of color. It is a difficult task to have the nation feel the same way about people of color as they did in the '60s. But there still exists persistent animosity towards them. Again here, I assume that my propaganda worked, and that there still exists enough racism to alienate people of color from the economy.

Dealing with so many unknowns is difficult. But let's assume that economic connections that exist now, remain exactly the same after all of my terrorism. This still will hurt people of color. The point of all of the attacks was to get the government to spend a trillion dollars. The economic divides that already exist will effectively direct that trillion dollars where the wealth already flows.

What if half of that trillion dollars is spent on communities of color? This could be bad news, as people of color won't feel animosity towards the government. I don't believe this will happen, but it's important to think of the possibilities. It would make my task longer, not harder. The streams of wealth that already exist in this country will simply absorb the wealth and the people of color would be in the same situation. Even still, there is no way this will happen, if history is a guide.

Now we have the dreaded relative deflation position. Almost anything is possible from such a position. It makes sense that I continue my random attacks to keep investors afraid. Then it will be time to step up the attacks.

Physical Attacks Against Outspoken Racists

There are scores of white Americans waiting for a race war. It is easy to find these anti-social individuals and attack them. This could possibly be a physical attack or a shooting. In the beginning, it would be important to keep them alive so they can talk about how angry they are. So if I were going to shoot one of these people, I would shoot them in the buttocks.

I would create a different group to taunt and harass "patriots." Guns are so easy to come by, and no matter how armed you are, you can't really "defend" yourself fast enough against a person who's stalking you. At this point, normal terrorists would be attacking police officers. That's silly, the police are hyper vigilant. Soft targets are the way to go; it's much easier to get away with.

What Will Happen?

This is essentially the end of my plan. I'm limited by the means available, and the structures in place to stop me. The point is to antagonize and economically isolate people of color and scare the rich into not spending money. There are many ways to achieve these goals, and I have put forth a few.

I assume that the people of color will be laid off at a higher rate than any other group during the recession. It is my hope that further terrorist activities and propaganda would increase that rate. I further assume that law enforcement will increase its antagonistic nature towards people of color. In addition to this, I assume that rich people will be far more concerned with making profits, or not losing money, than the state of the nation. I assume that my tactics will scare them enough to not spend.

Next, the go-to move for the Federal Government has never, and will never, directly affect ordinary people. If enough people are disconnected from the economy, then the increased spending will create areas of relative deflation.

Finally, antagonizing white supremacists could be the final straw. Why? Because they will find cause to counter-attack communities of color. Maybe mass shootings, maybe church burning, and maybe much more. This will be the final straw for people of color as it will seem as if the police aren't protecting them. I personally don't feel safe around police. I don't think I'm alone in my feelings. People attacking communities of color are simply out of the police's hands. They can only do so much. But the sentiment will be anti-police anyhow.

I hope to recreate the black uprisings of the past. If that happens, it doesn't make sense to continue my terrorist activities.

Won't the Uprising Fail?

America has the strongest military in the world. There is no chance that there will be any sustained uprisings in America. Also, considering a good portion of the military are minorities, genocide is highly unlikely. If history is a good guide, what will happen is an uptick in arrests and convictions. This is my ultimate goal.

America has progressed to the moment where she has forgotten why she's imprisoned so many people of color in the first place. The prison-industrial complex was a direct result of black uprisings in the past. Now that the uprisings have subsided dramatically, America is finally talking about reducing its inmate population.

The eyesore that is the prison industry is a cancer that could cripple the America economy. It is a great fortune that the industry is subsidized by slave labor. Dramatically increasing the prison population will have extreme effects on the economy. The first effect is the direct cost of incarceration to the taxpayers. Next is the economic losses suffered to communities of color as more people are removed from the economy. Finally is the competitive cost to businesses that are unable to compete with slave labor.

The prison system is another economic choke point in the nation. It is a self-perpetuating organism. The only thing it succeeds in doing is creating further economic imbalances and hurting the nation economically.

You Don't Believe

Some of you reading this will deny the possibilities. In fact, some of you will deny that racism even exists. Some of you will believe that "American ingenuity" will save the day. You may even believe that there are people out there that won't allow any of this. For those of you who doubt, I want you to understand that our nation has had a plethora of economic collapses. Each economic collapse was just as mysterious as the next one.

The economic collapses of the past are no mystery to me. They happen when wealth stops circulating. It is a rapid cascade effect that appears, to some, as a natural disaster. Unfortunately, they are far more predictable than some would like to admit.

In all honesty, it doesn't really matter if the plan would work or not. The truth is, the inevitable is rushing towards us and no one is the wiser. Almost any significant technological advance will do all the work that I just laid out.

Let's say we discover a way to extend human life by fifty years, but it costs a half a million dollars. That would create the same effects as having a contagious disease. Health care costs would dramatically shoot up, creating stark economic imbalances. How about this? How long before technology makes half of the jobs prisoners do obsolete? How long before this happens? Ten or Twenty years?? That would make for a hell of an economic problem.

Finally, we have the driverless car. I in fact did end with this. The driverless car isn't a hypothetical; it's happening right now. It's mind-boggling that I'm the only one that I know that is insanely troubled at the thought of it. The driverless car will lay bare all of our stupid economic policies.

THE END

Thank you for reading my book. It was a personal challenge for me to share, and honestly I feel quite good about it. If you enjoyed this book, please feel free to write a book review on Amazon, Goodreads, Barnes & Nobles, or any other bookseller you think is important.

Please follow me @HarlemGray, and visit my website at www. StopNYSlavery.com.

Thank you again and I hope we can change the world together.

www.ingramcontent.com/pod-product-compliance
Lightning Source LLC
Chambersburg PA
CBHW021904020426
42334CB00013B/469